I0426956

Welcome to a prehistoric journey where the past comes alive on the pages of this enchanting coloring book! Unleash your creativity and embark on an adventure through the mesmerizing world of dinosaurs. Roam the lush landscapes where mighty T-Rexes rule, graceful Velociraptors dart through the foliage, and gentle herbivores graze in serene valleys. In this captivating coloring experience, you have the power to bring these ancient creatures to life with every stroke of your pencil or splash of color. Get ready to dive into a realm where imagination meets history, and where your artistic expressions will resurrect the wonders of the dinosaur era. Let the coloring expedition begin!

Ricardo Silveira

2024

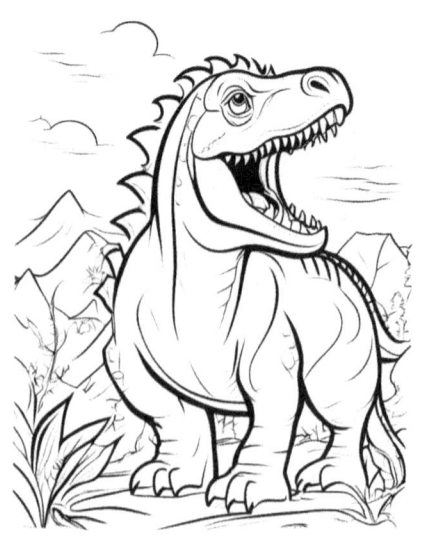 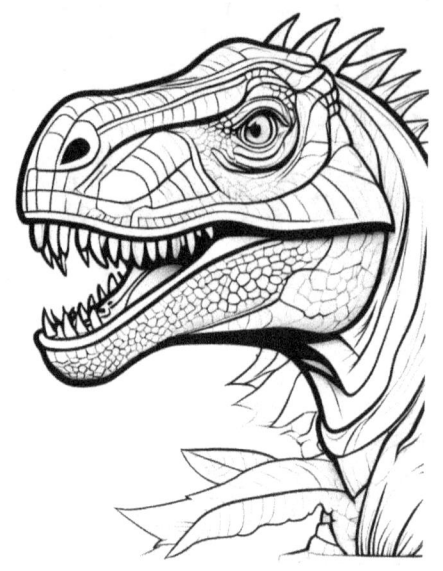

This Book Belongs to:

○─────────────────────────────────────○

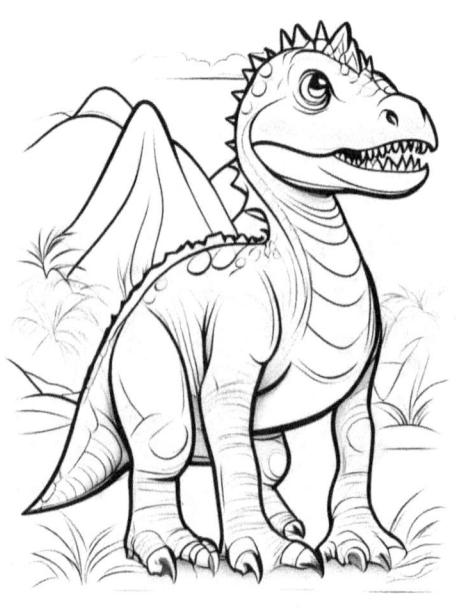 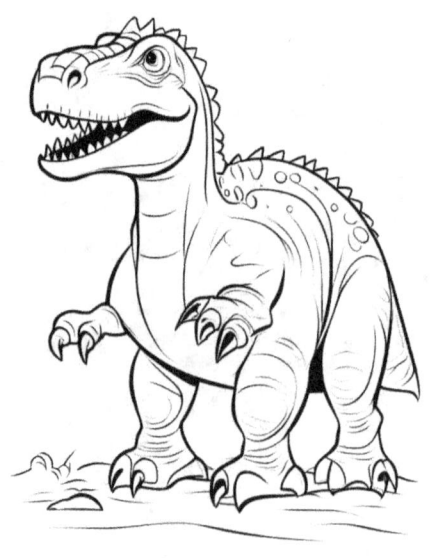

Test Color Page

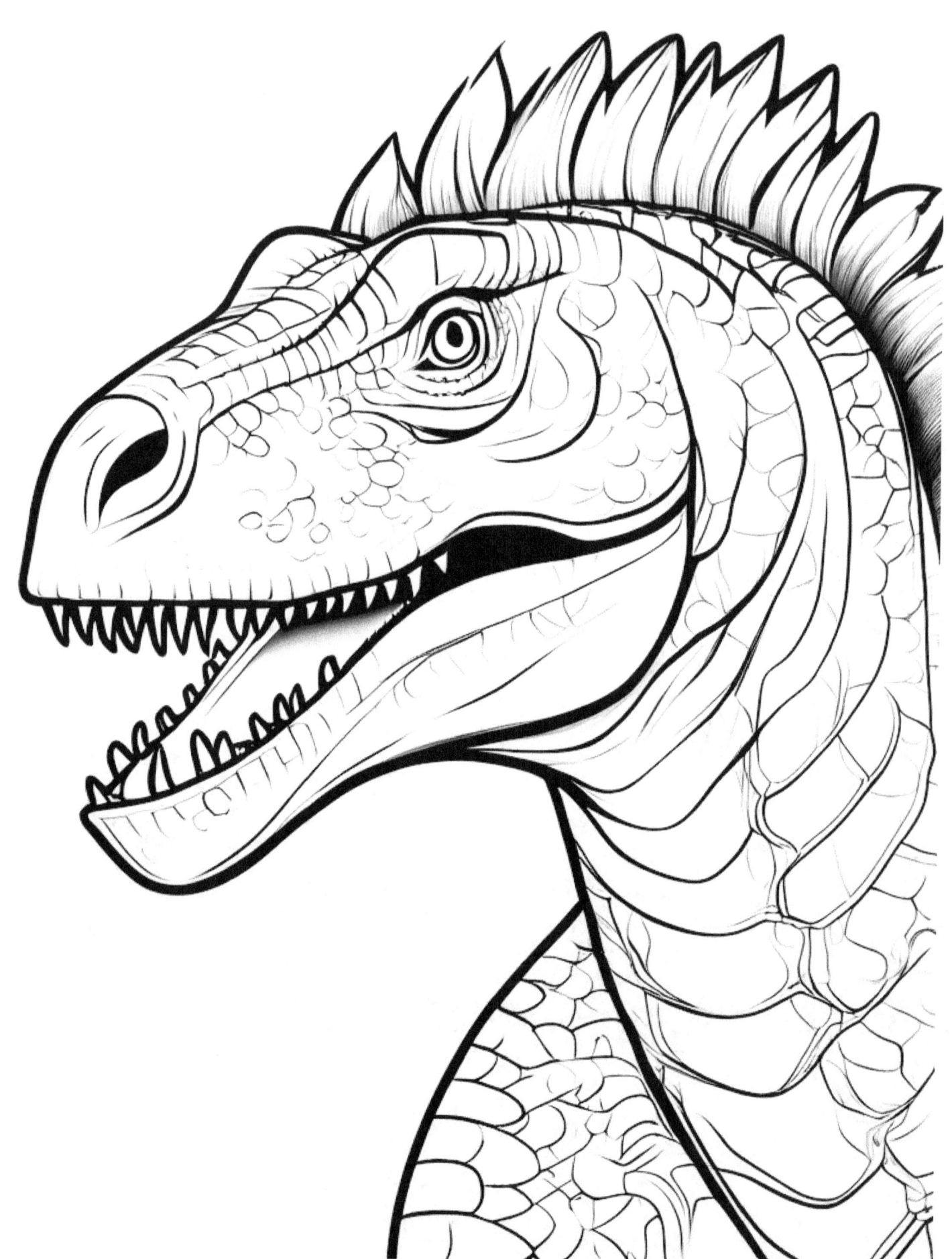

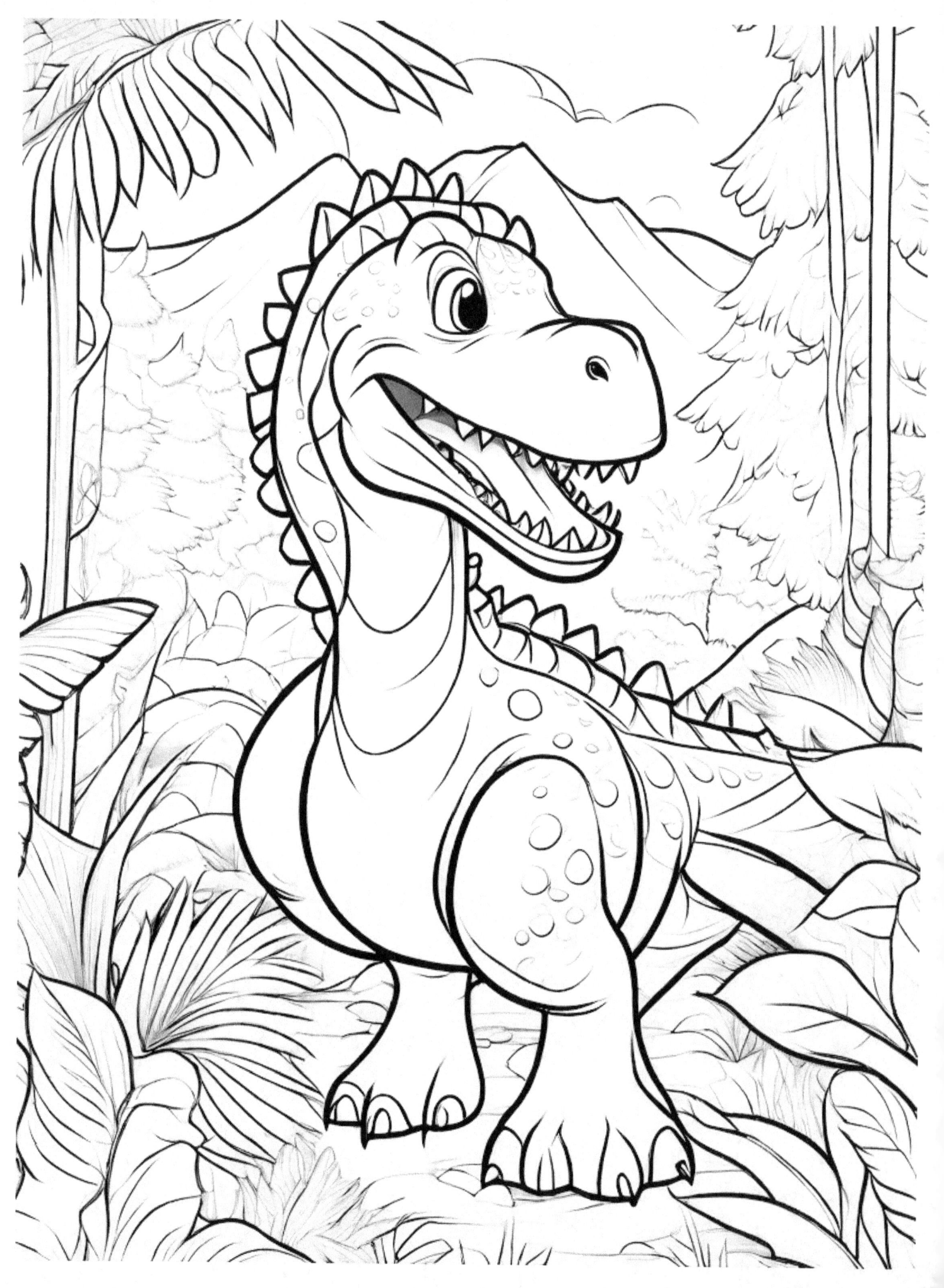

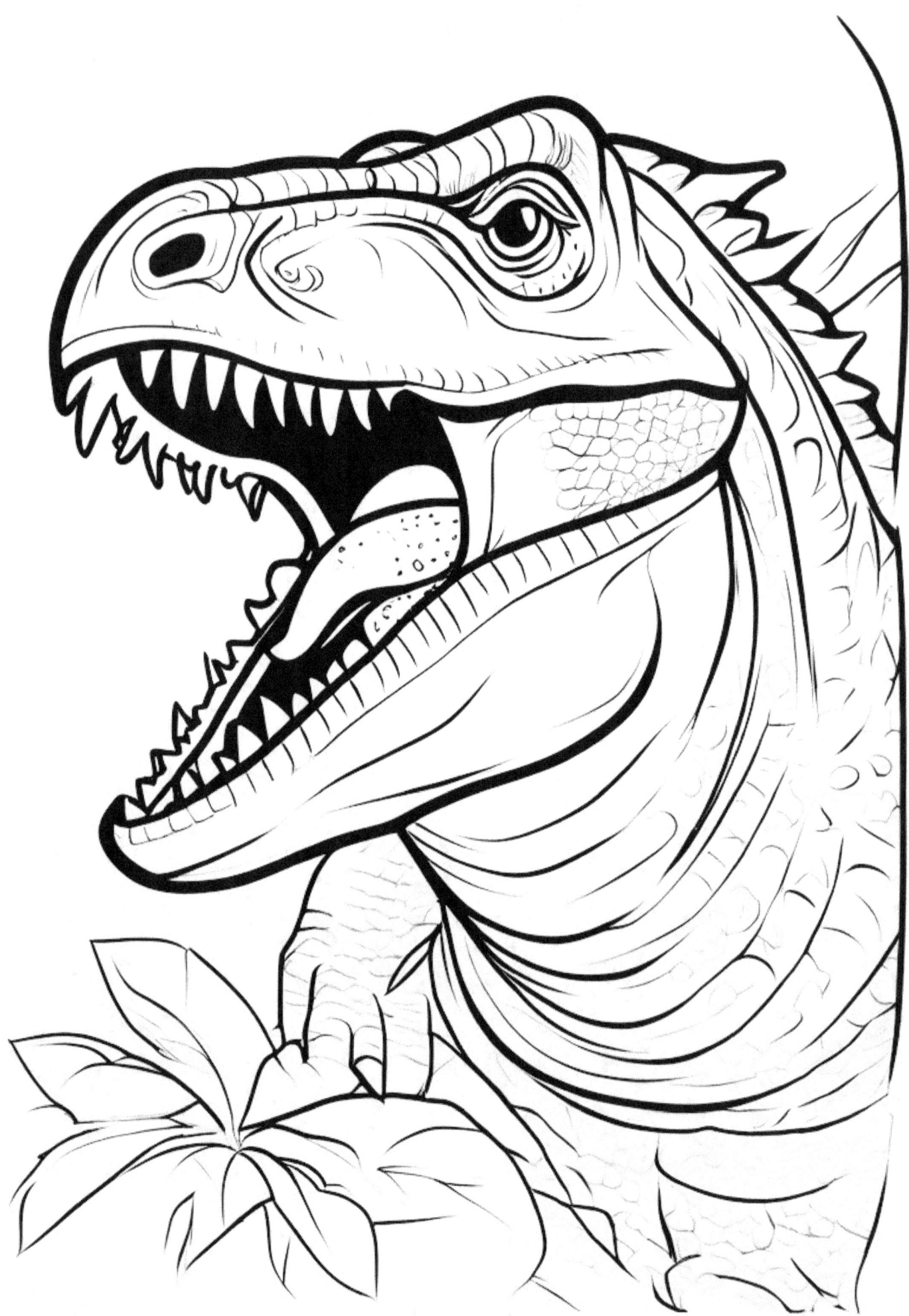

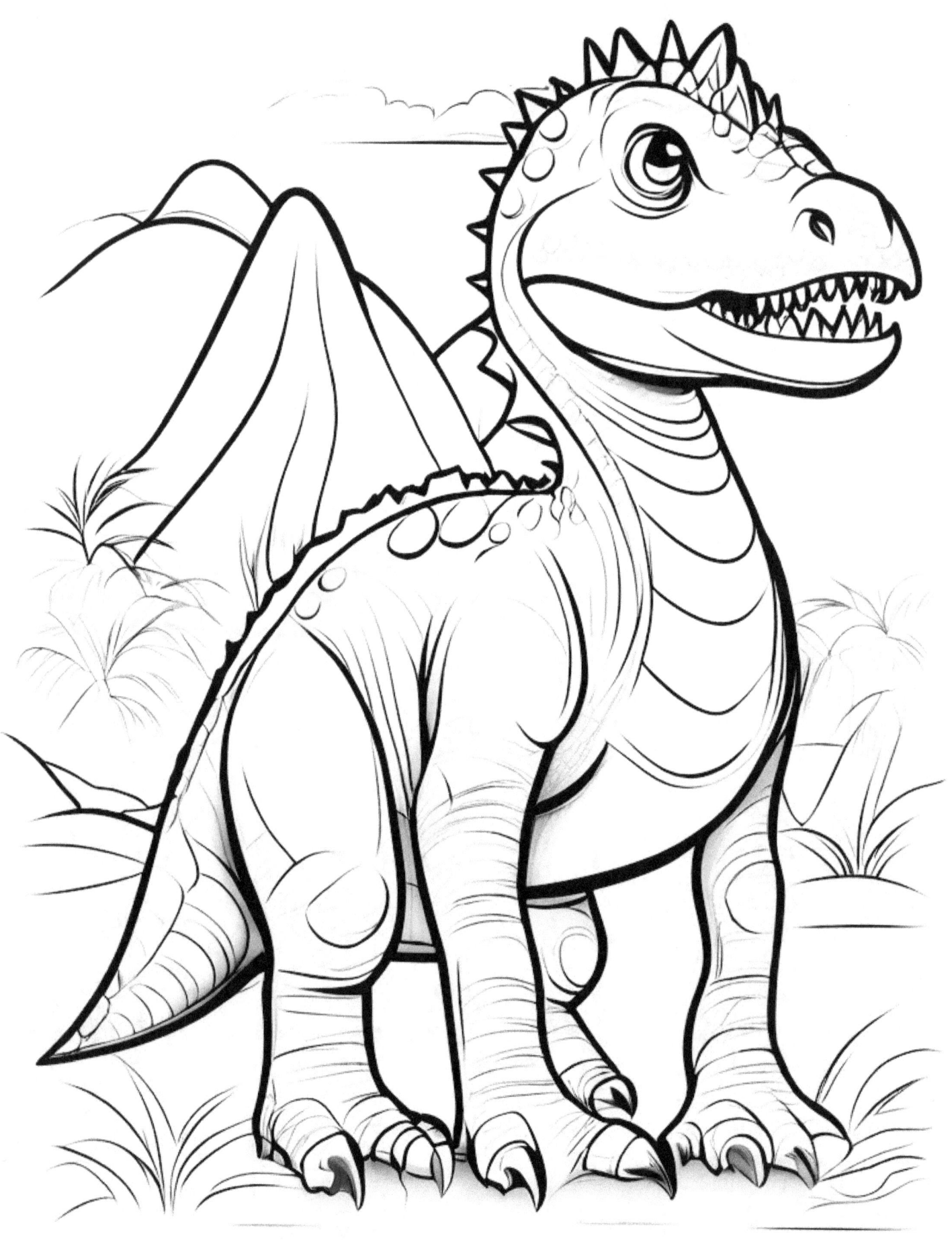

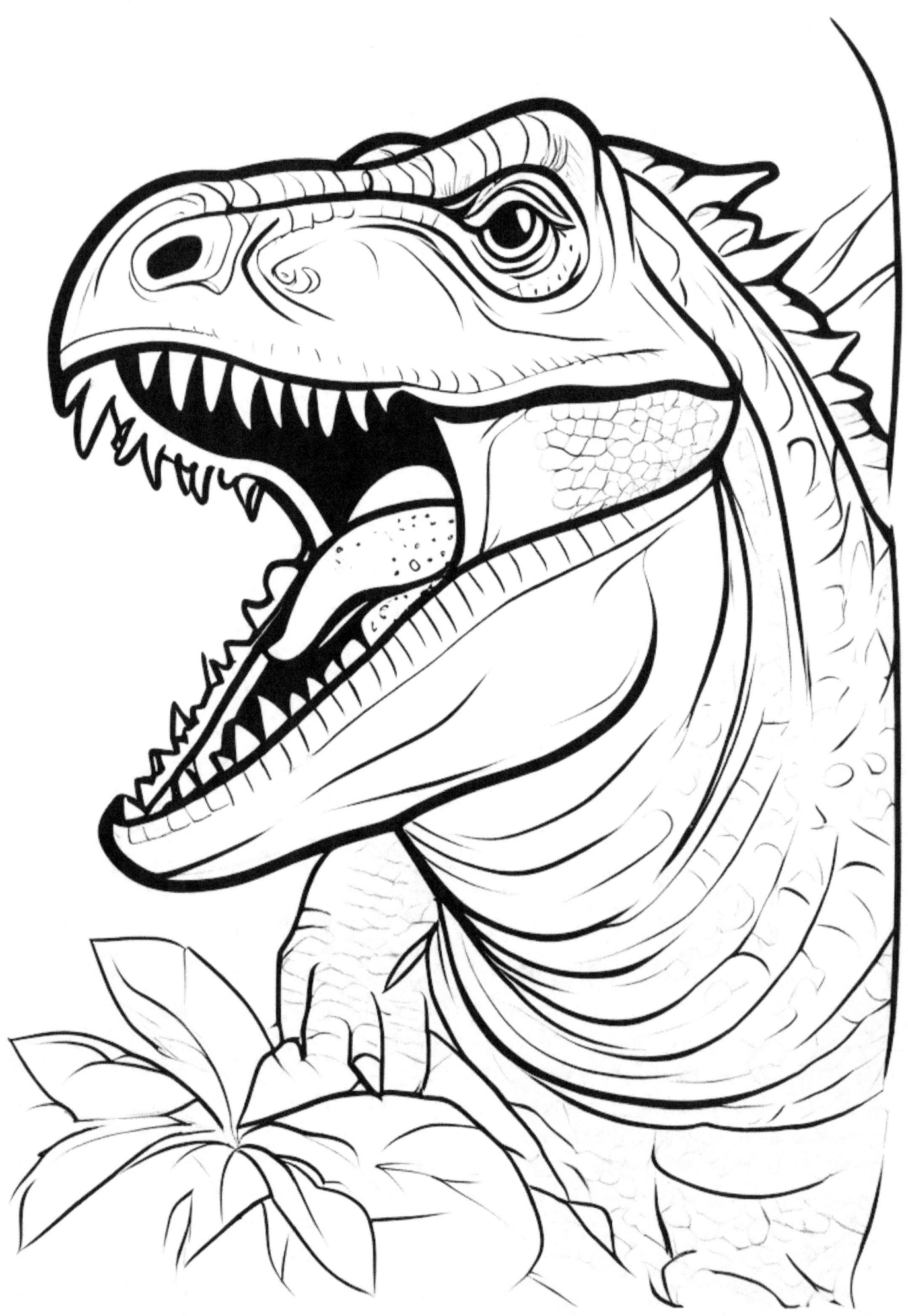

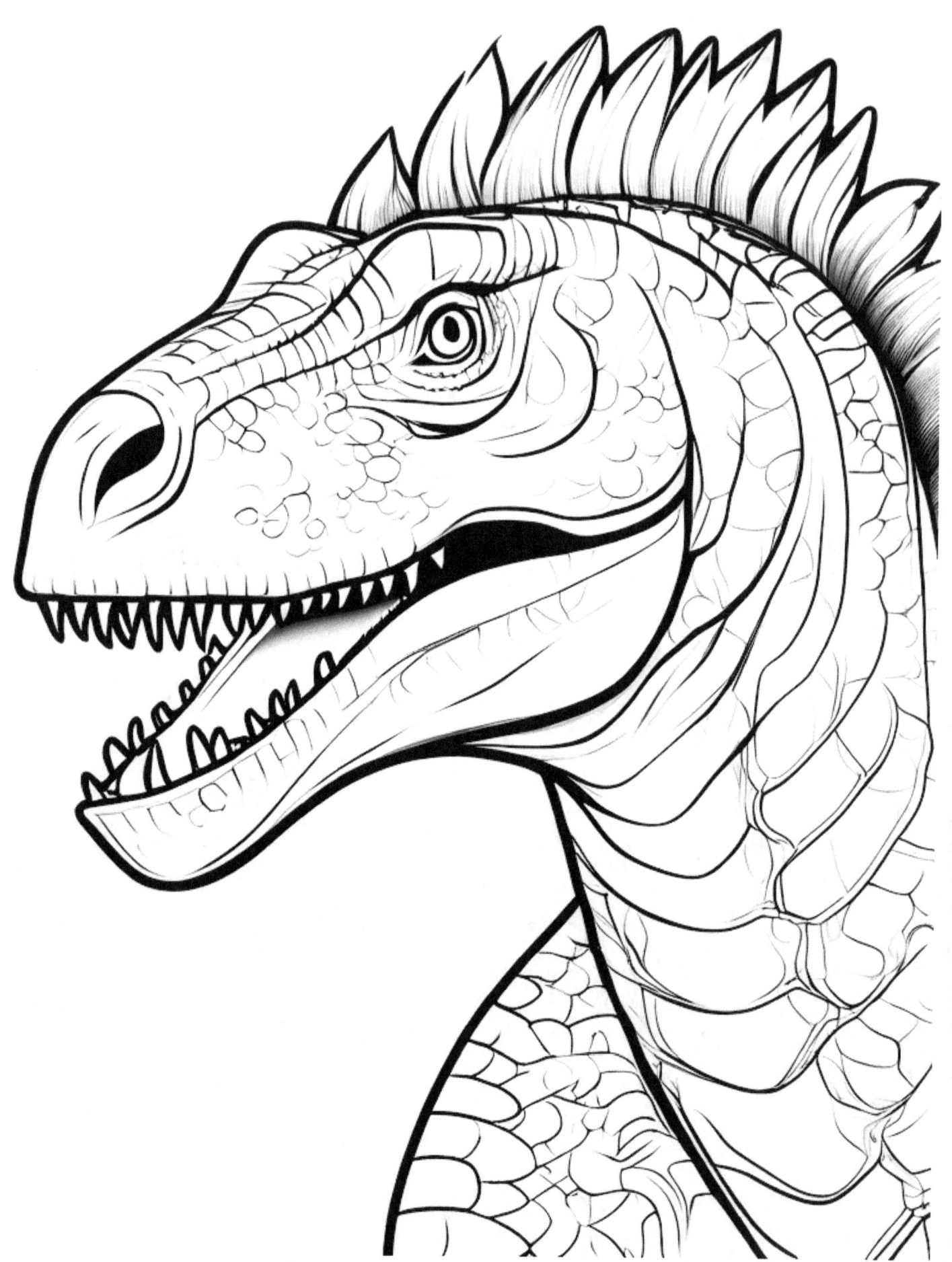

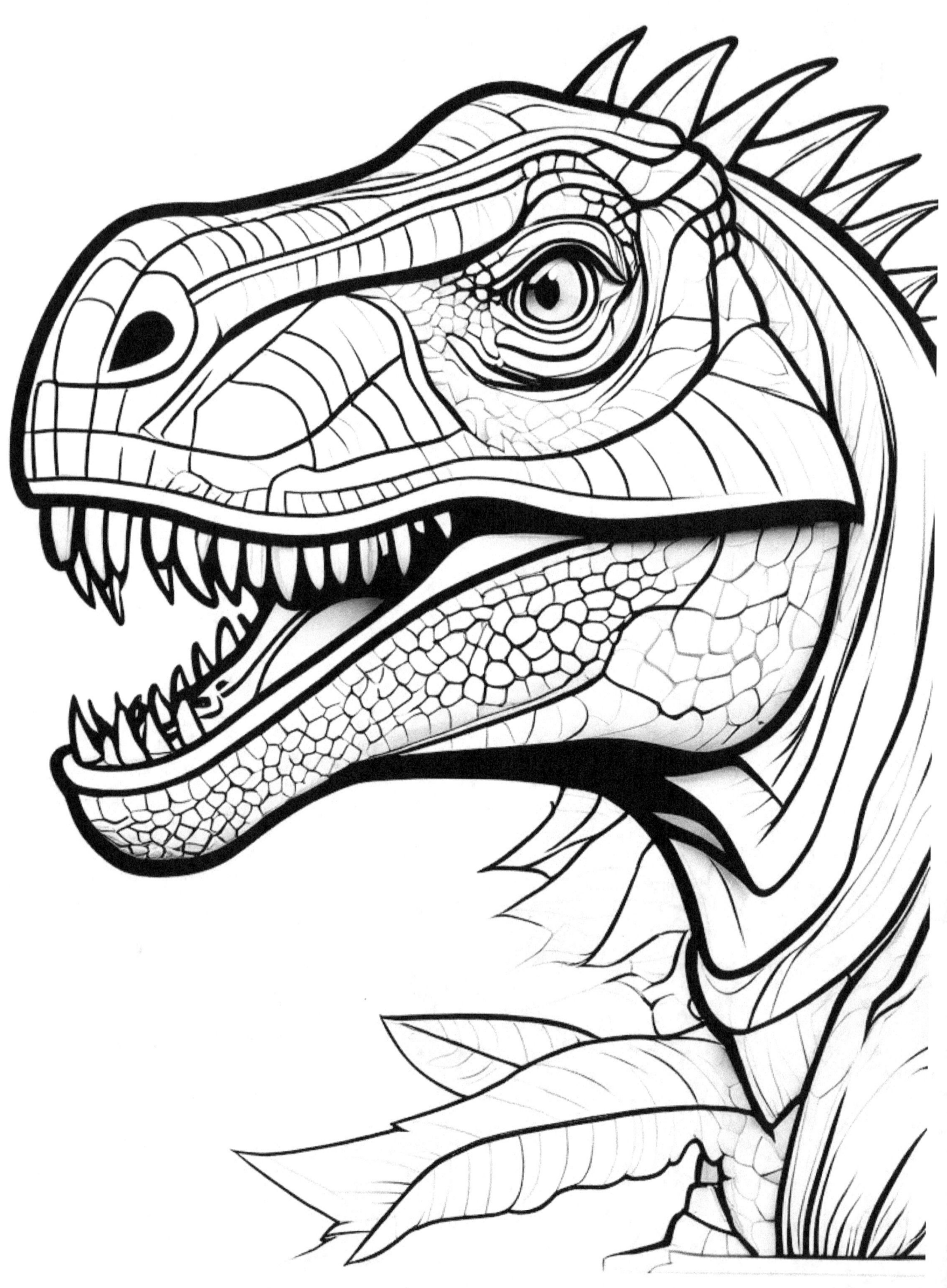

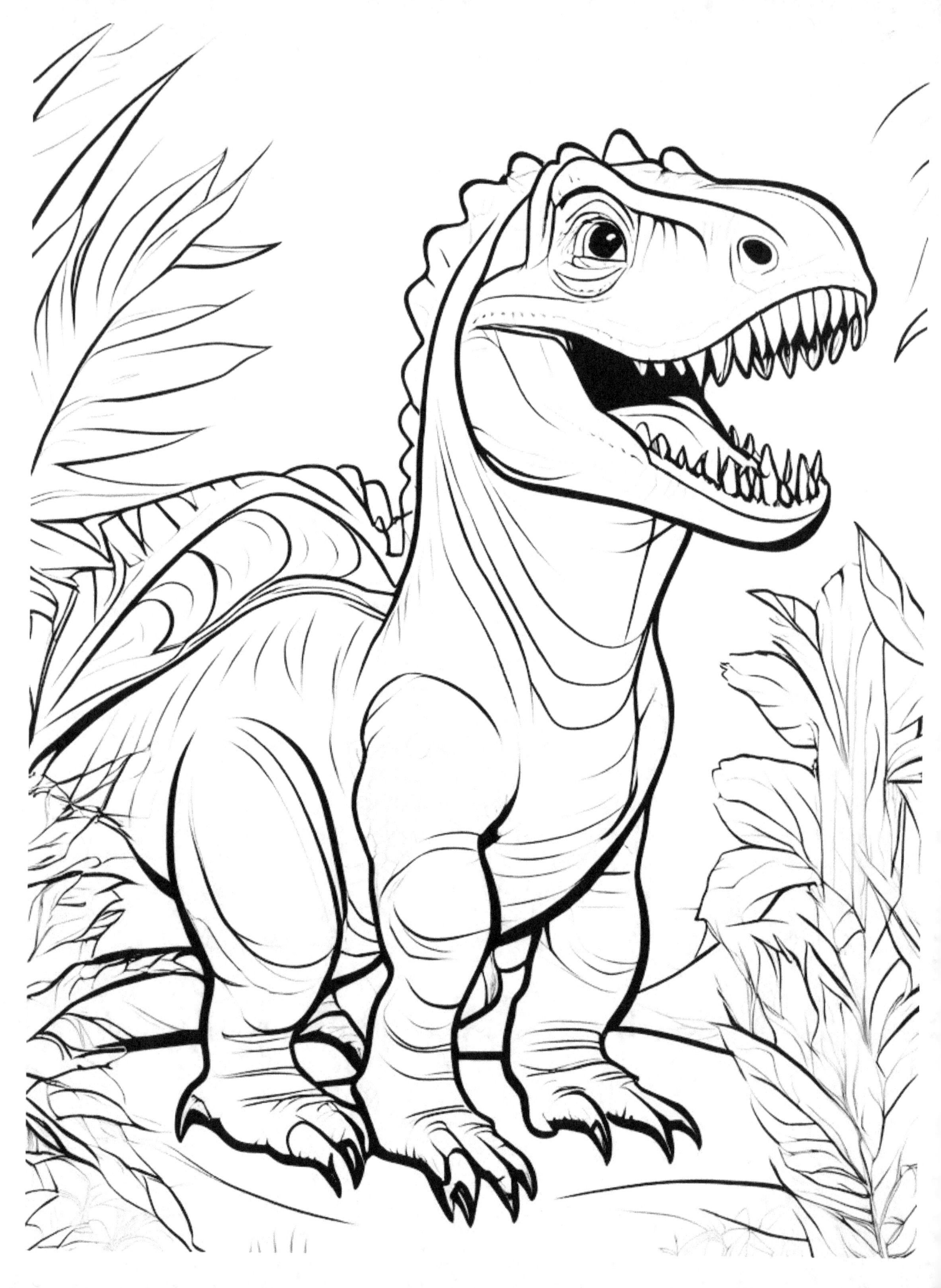

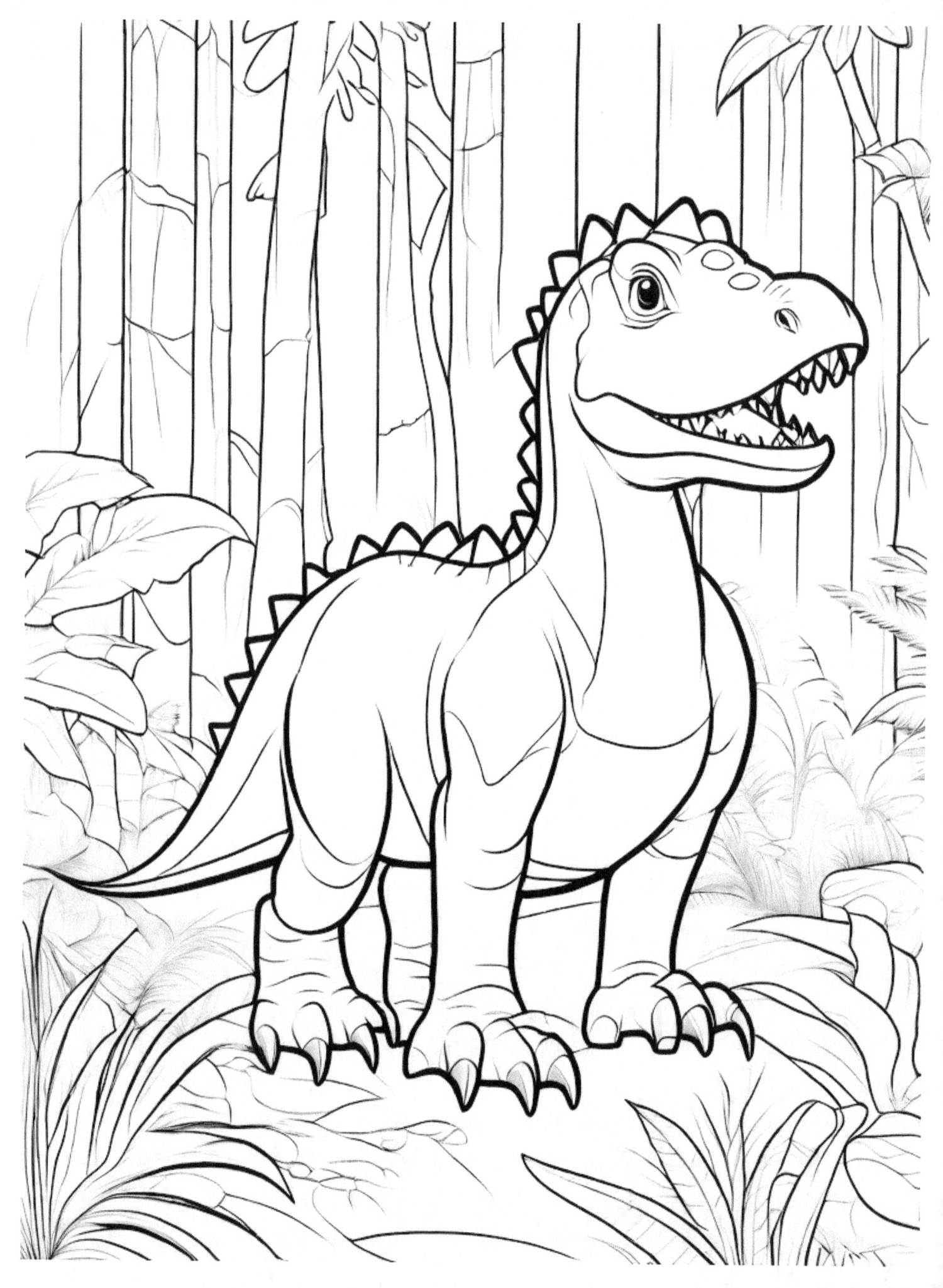

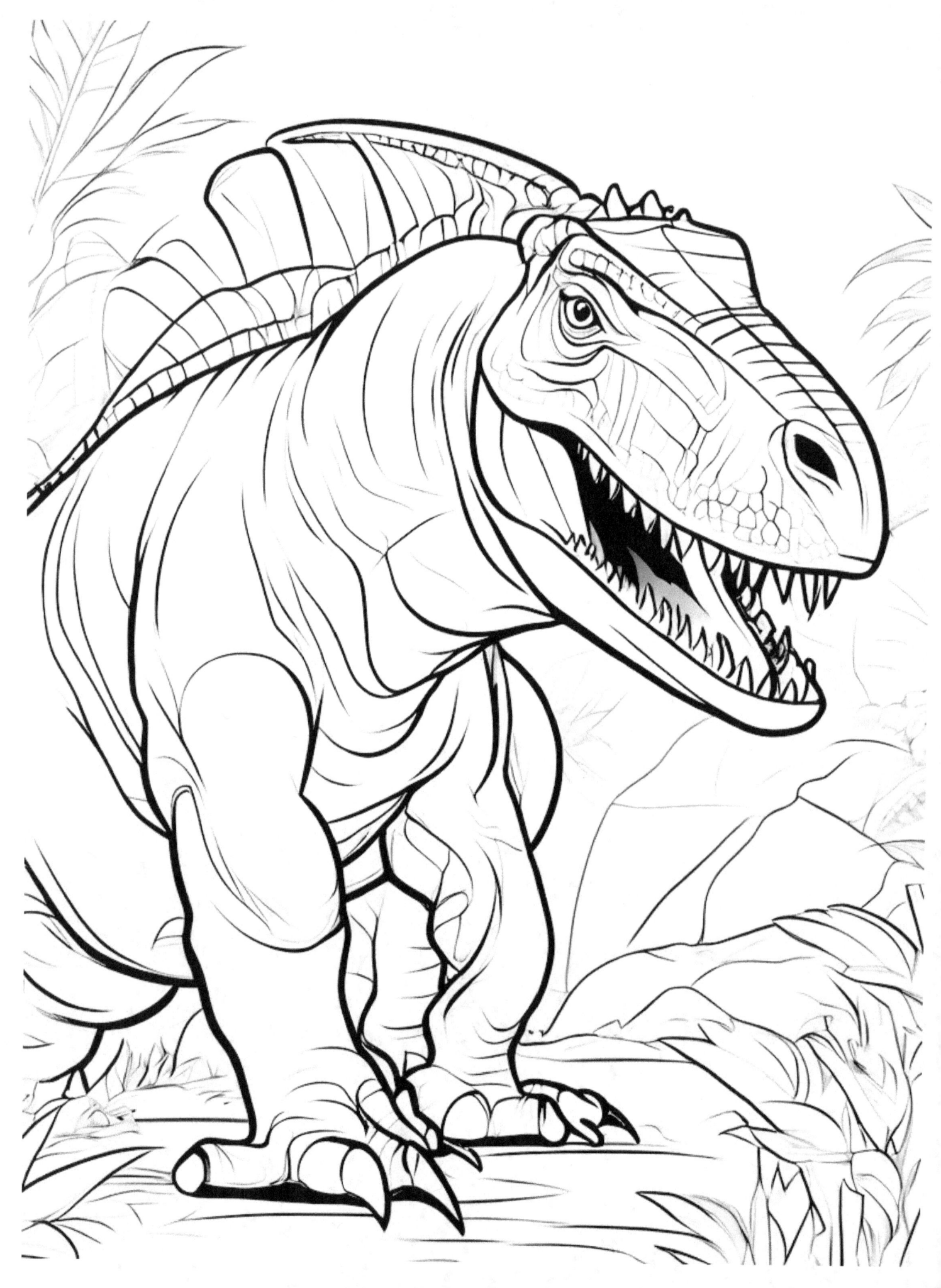

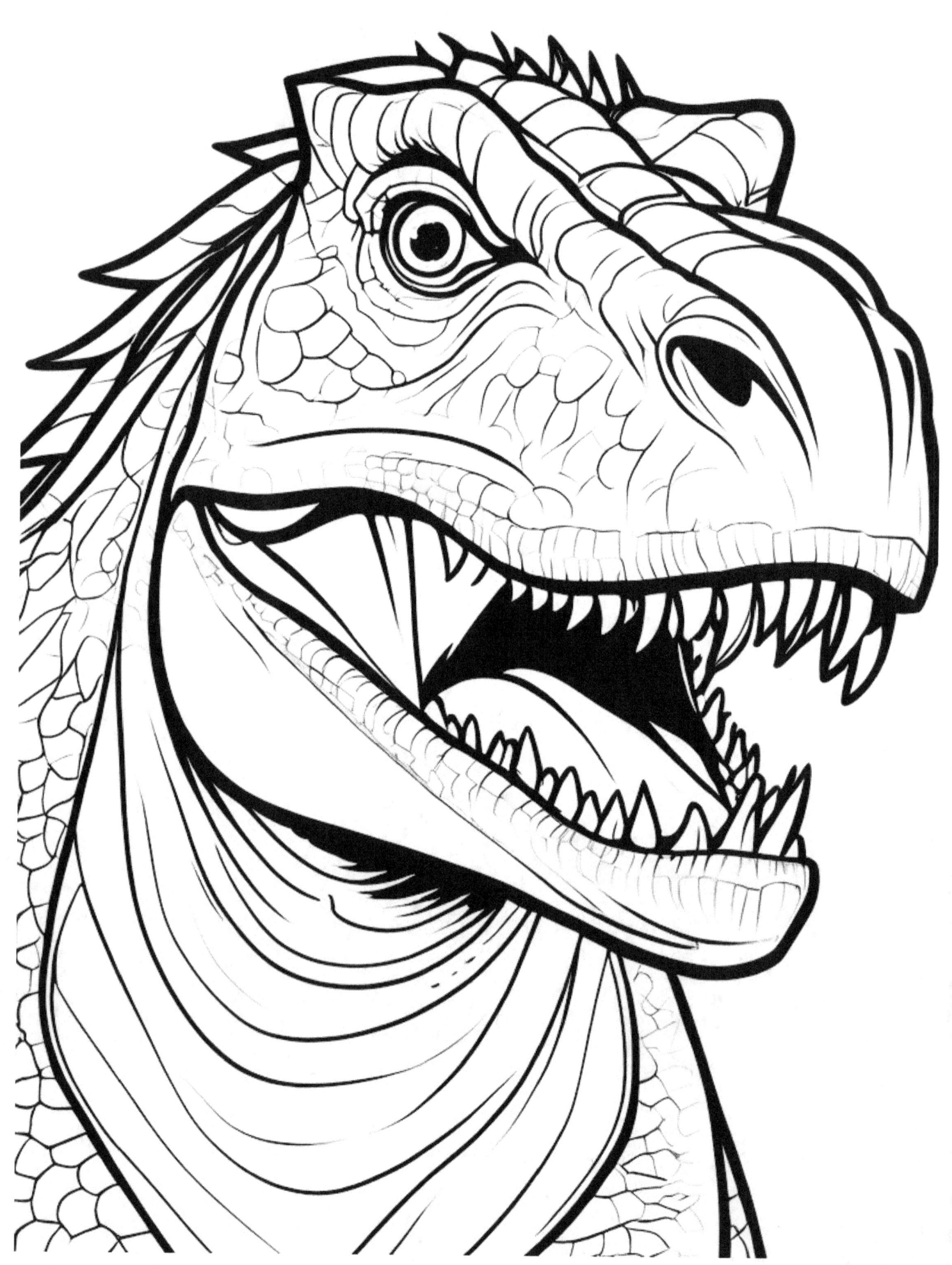

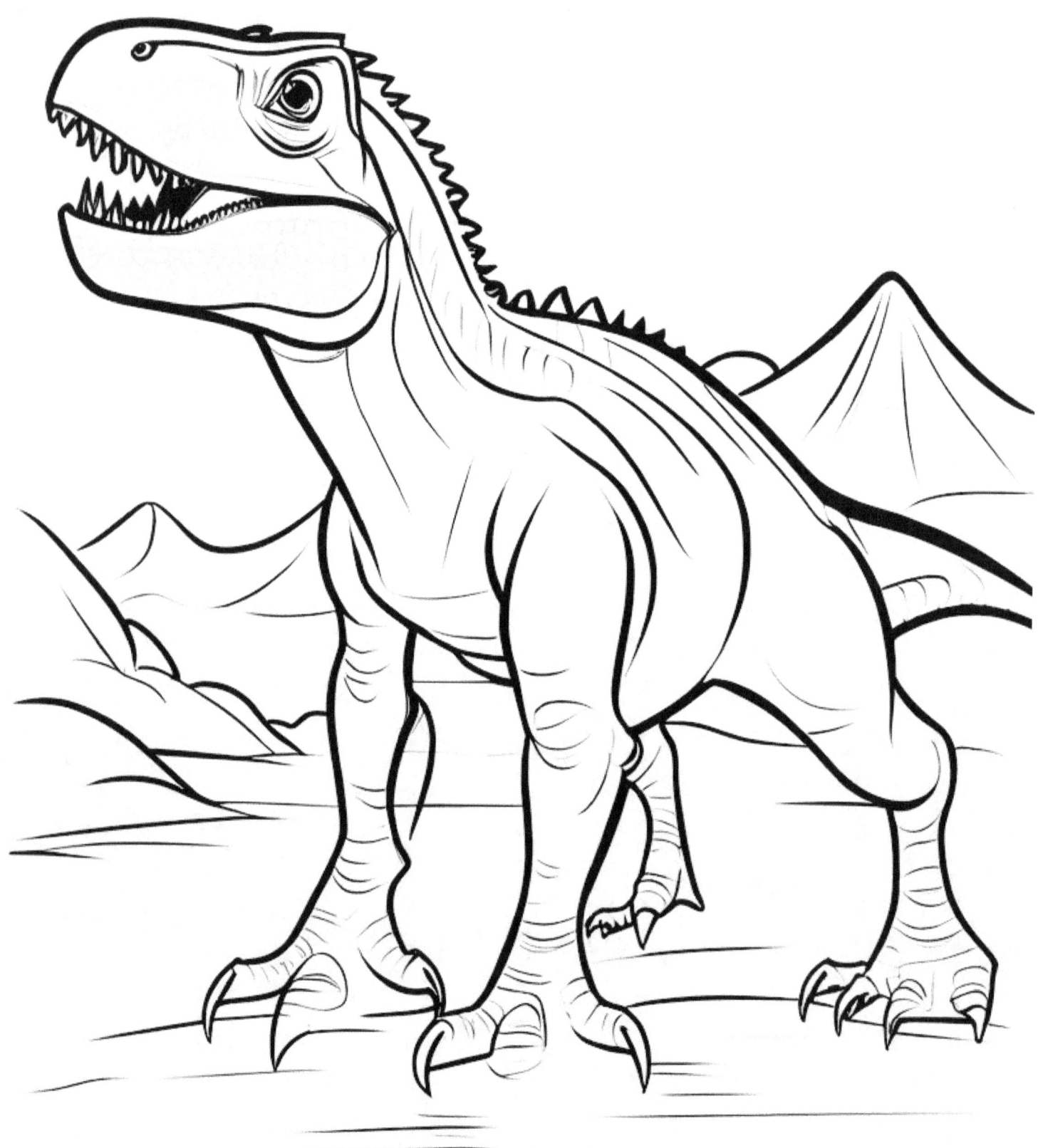

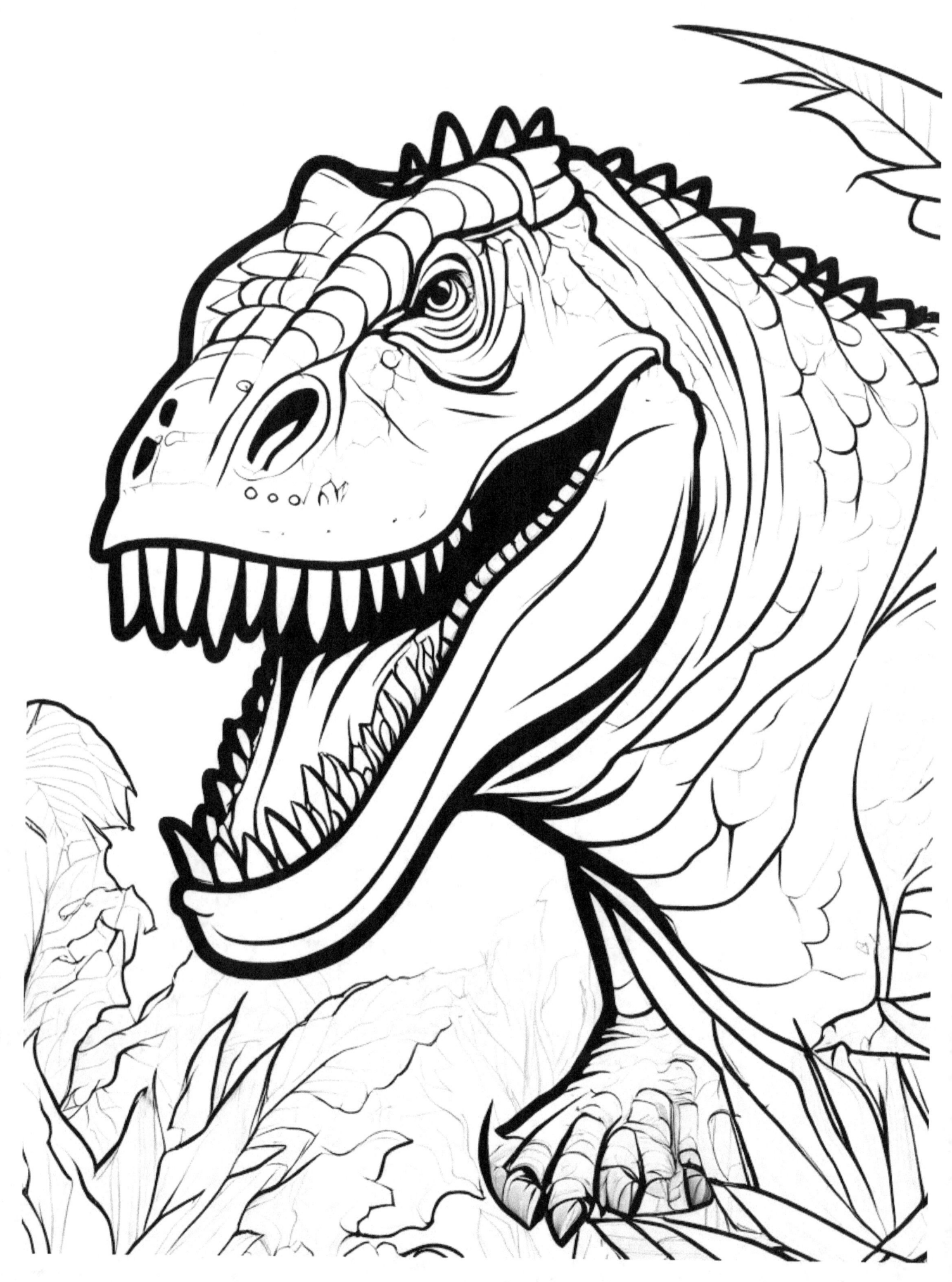

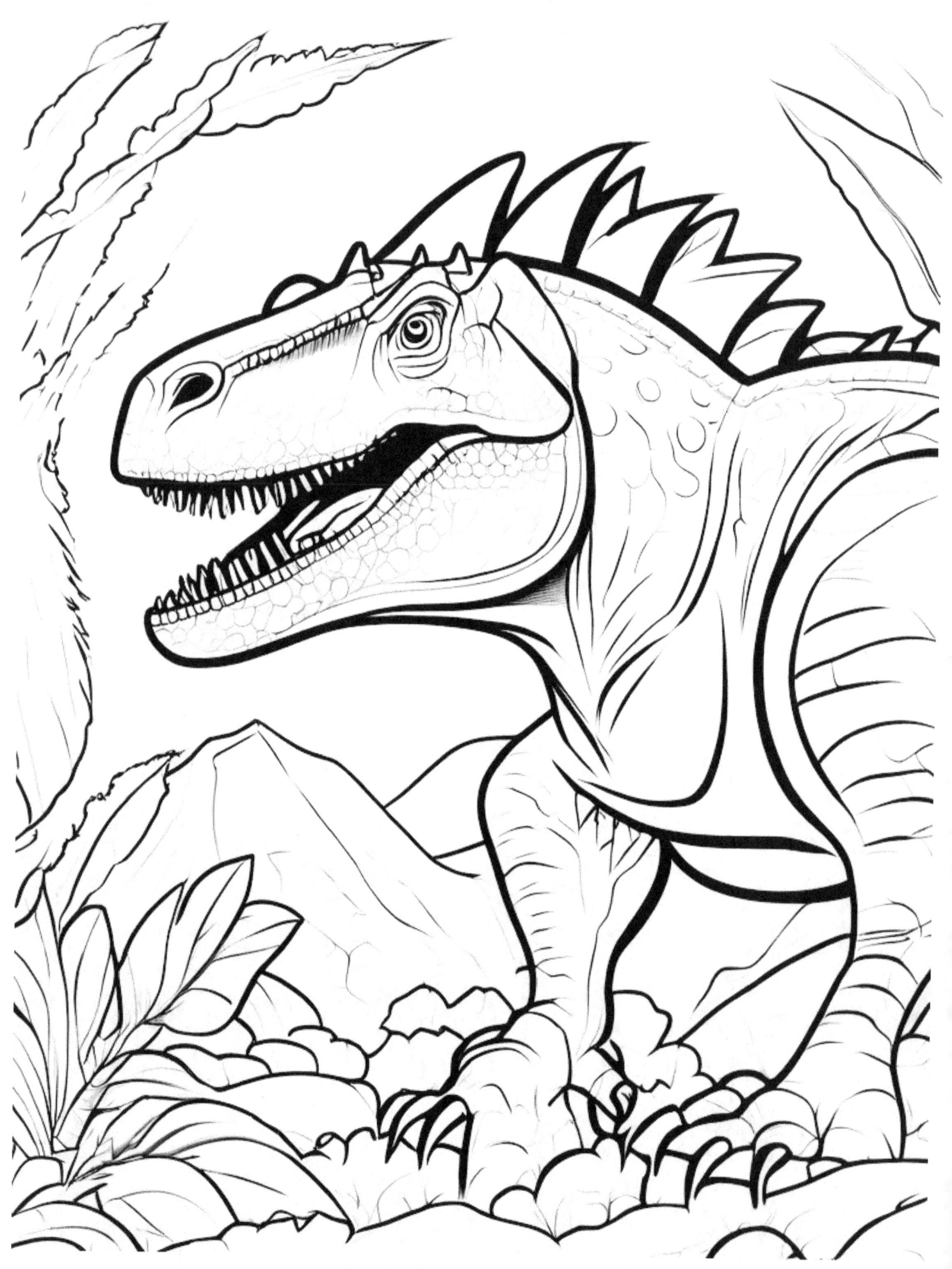

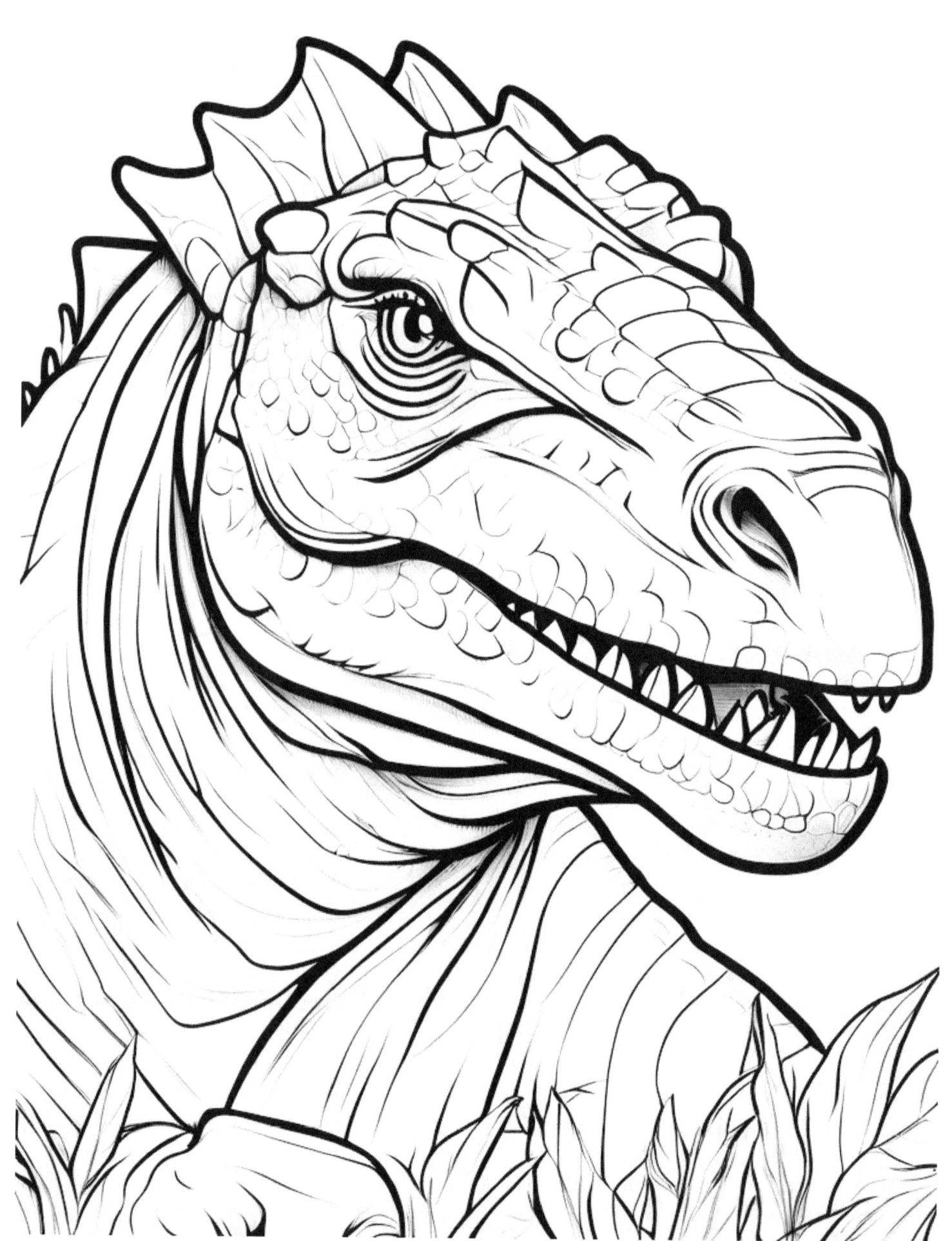

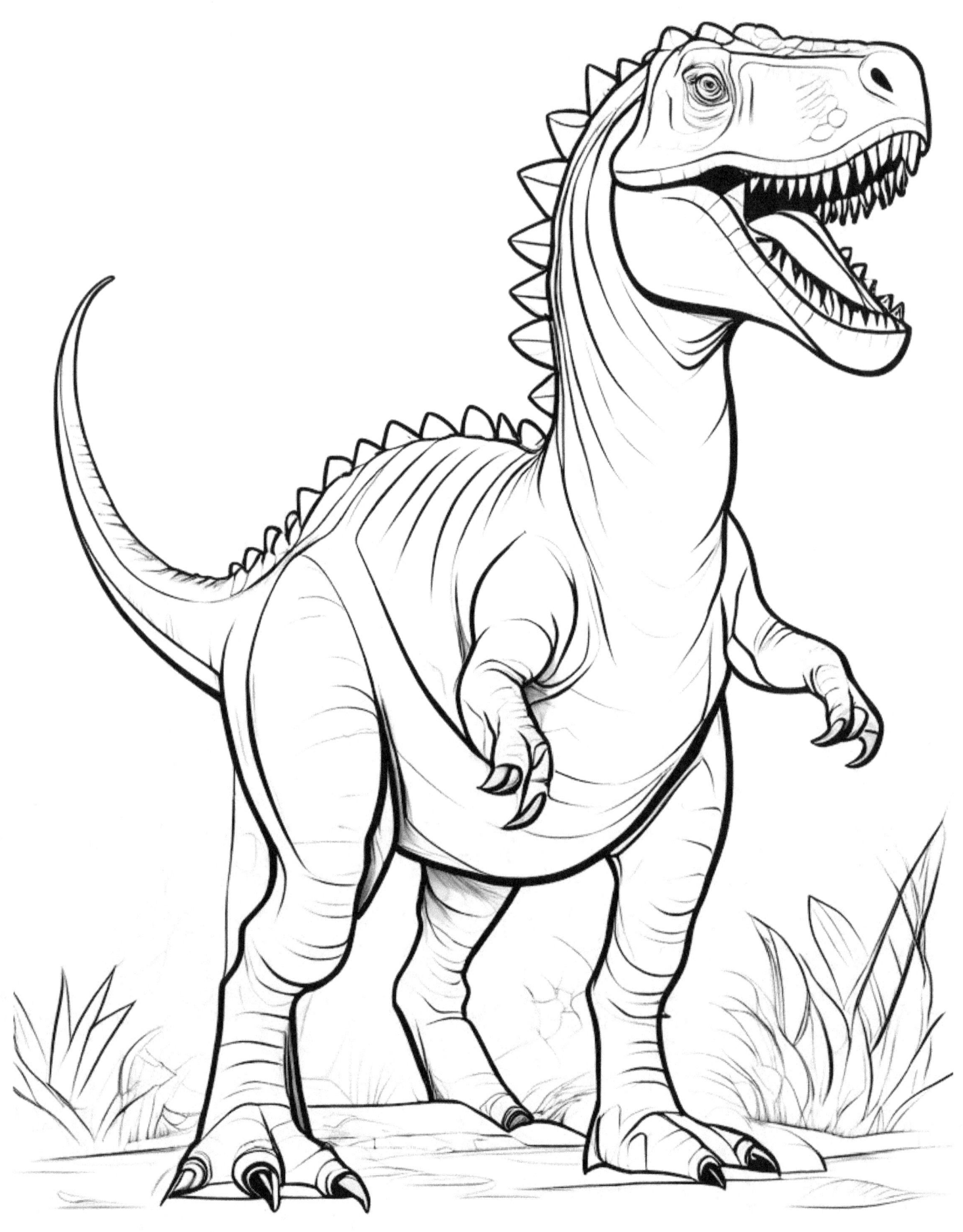

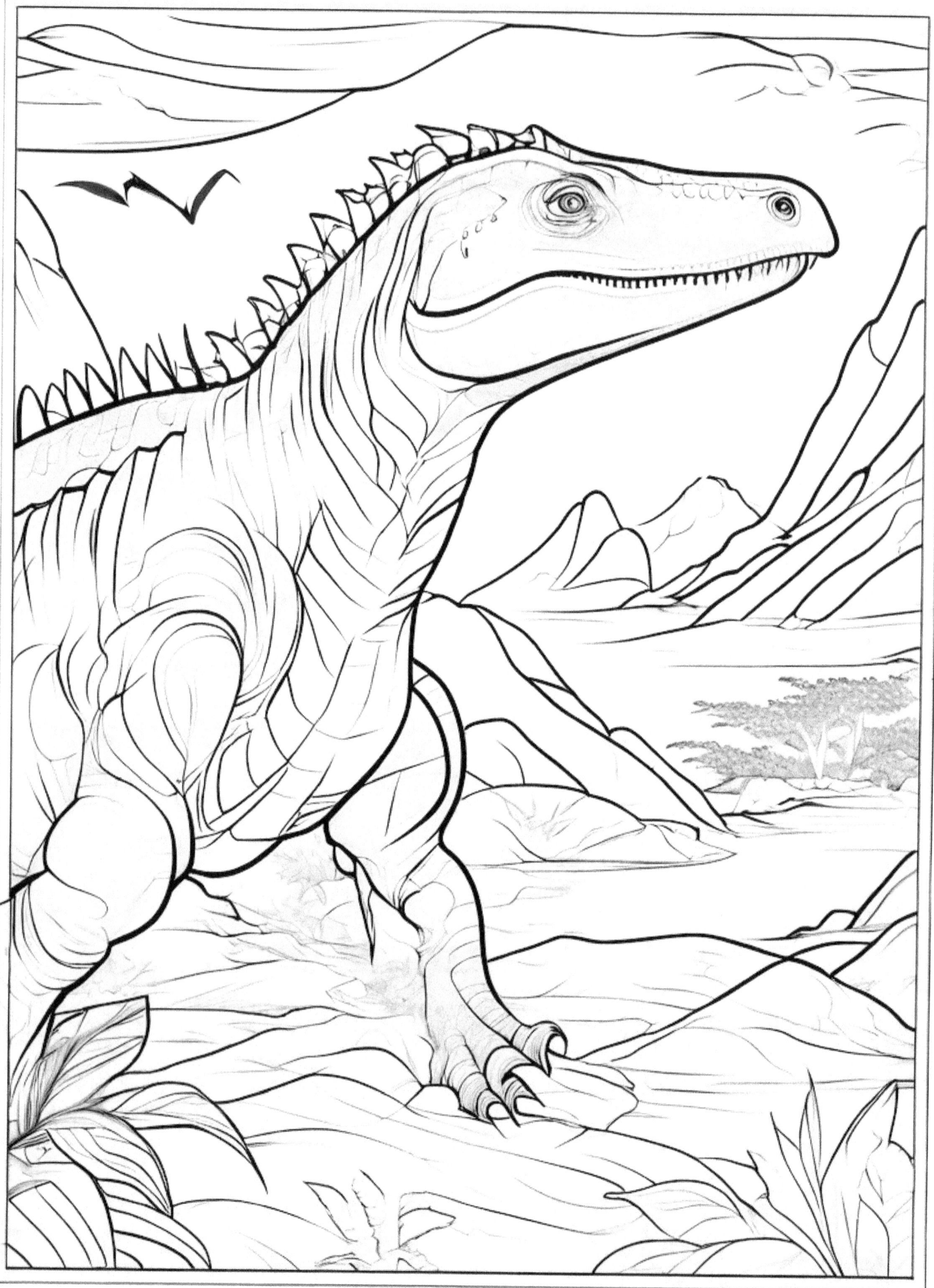

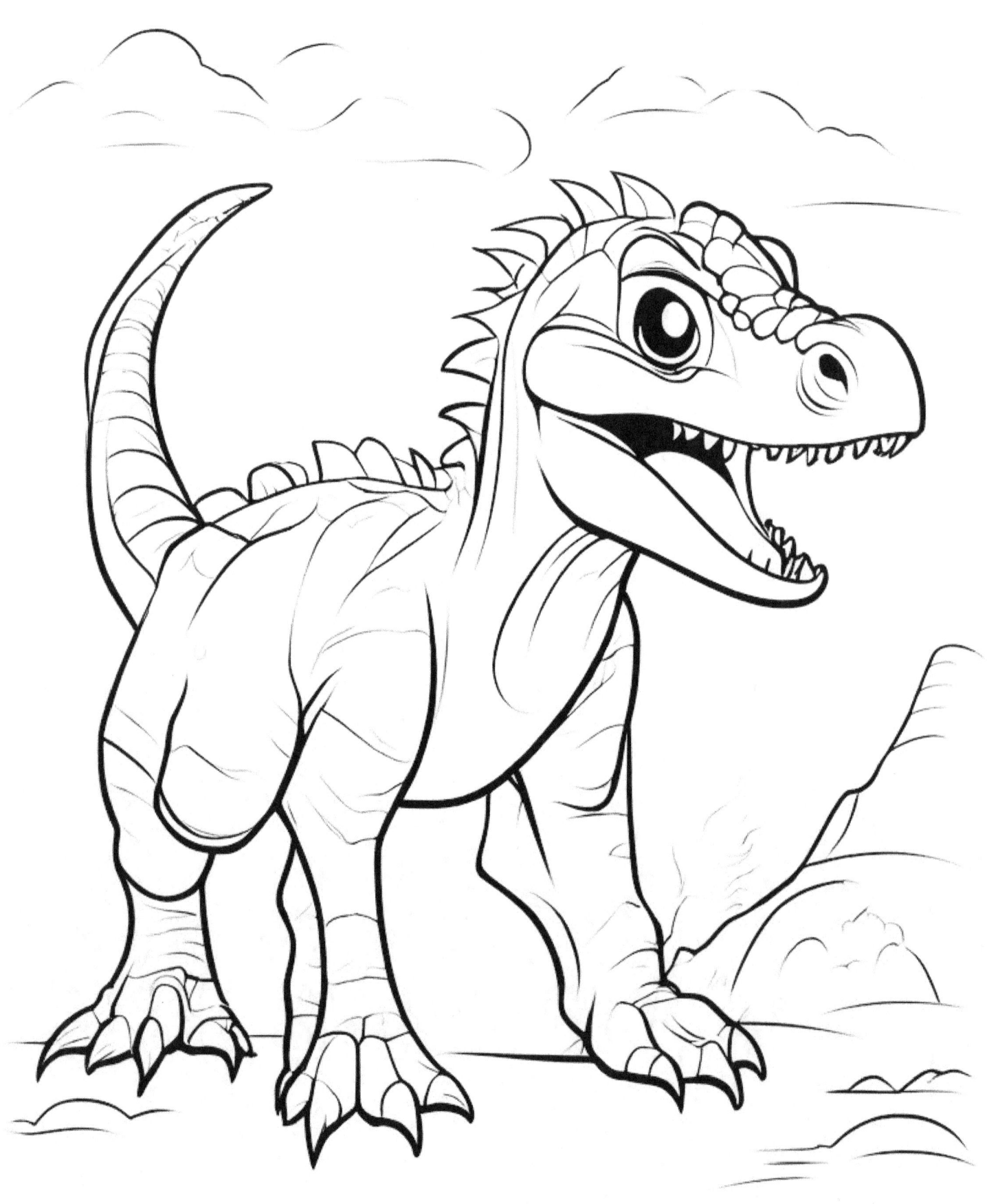

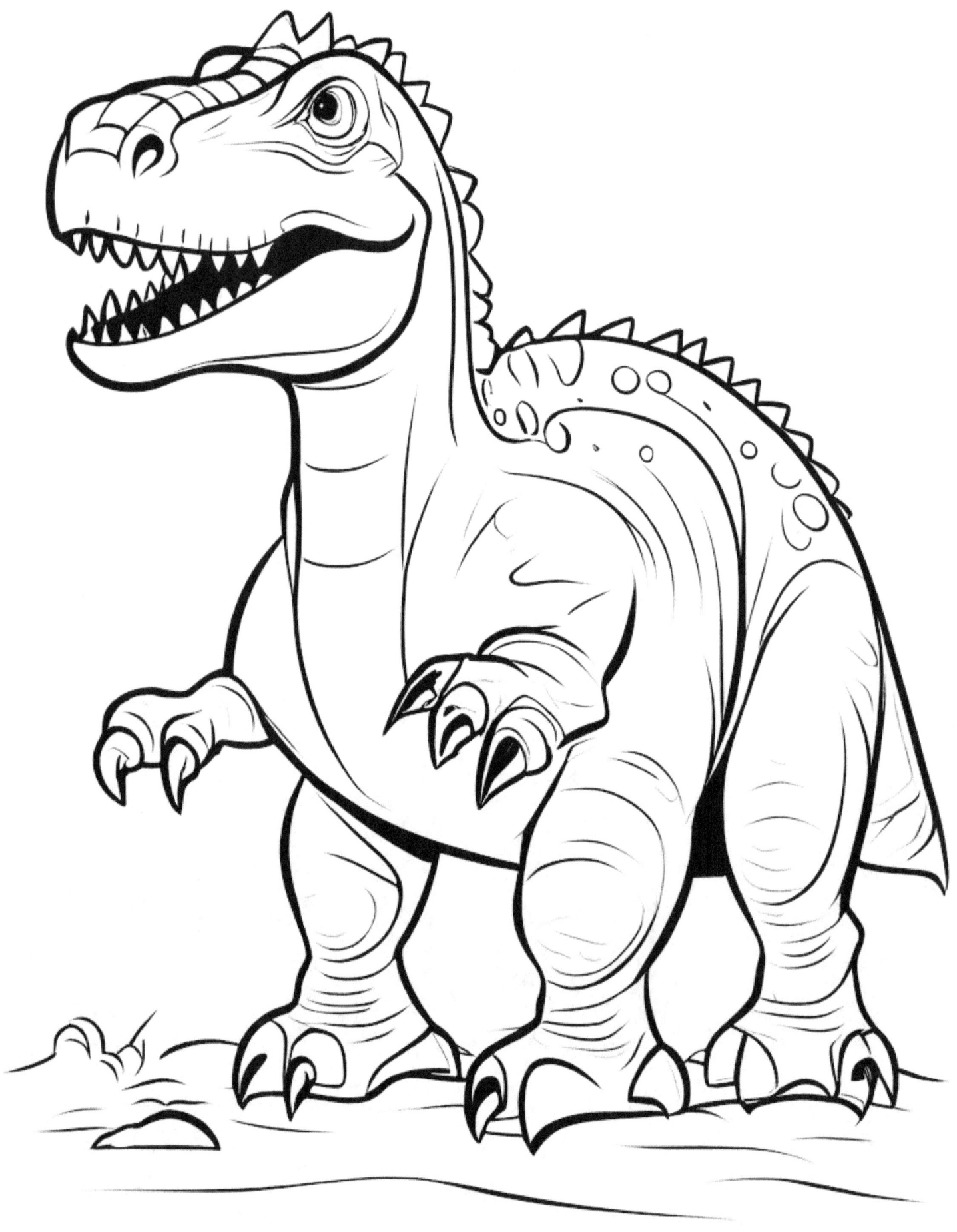

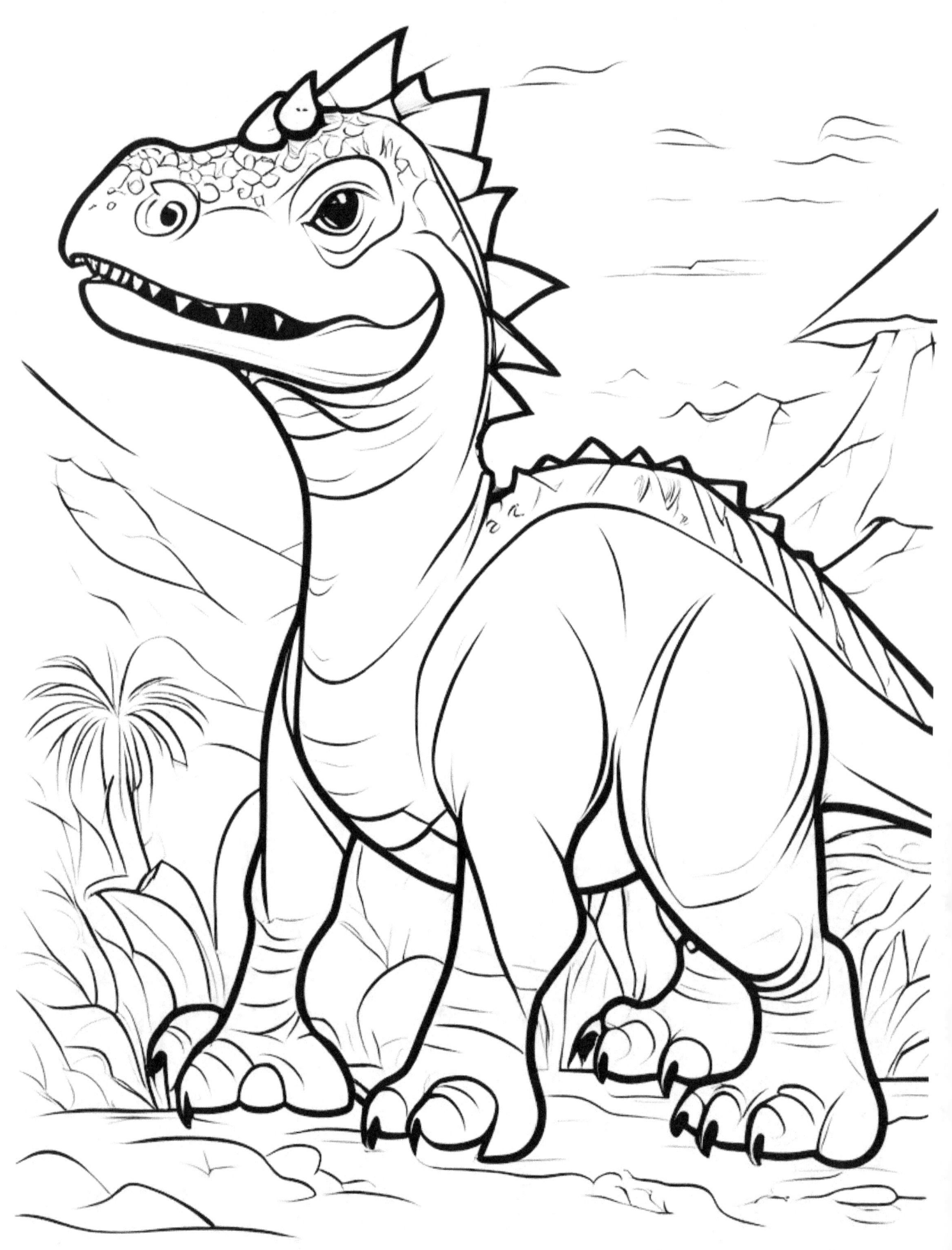

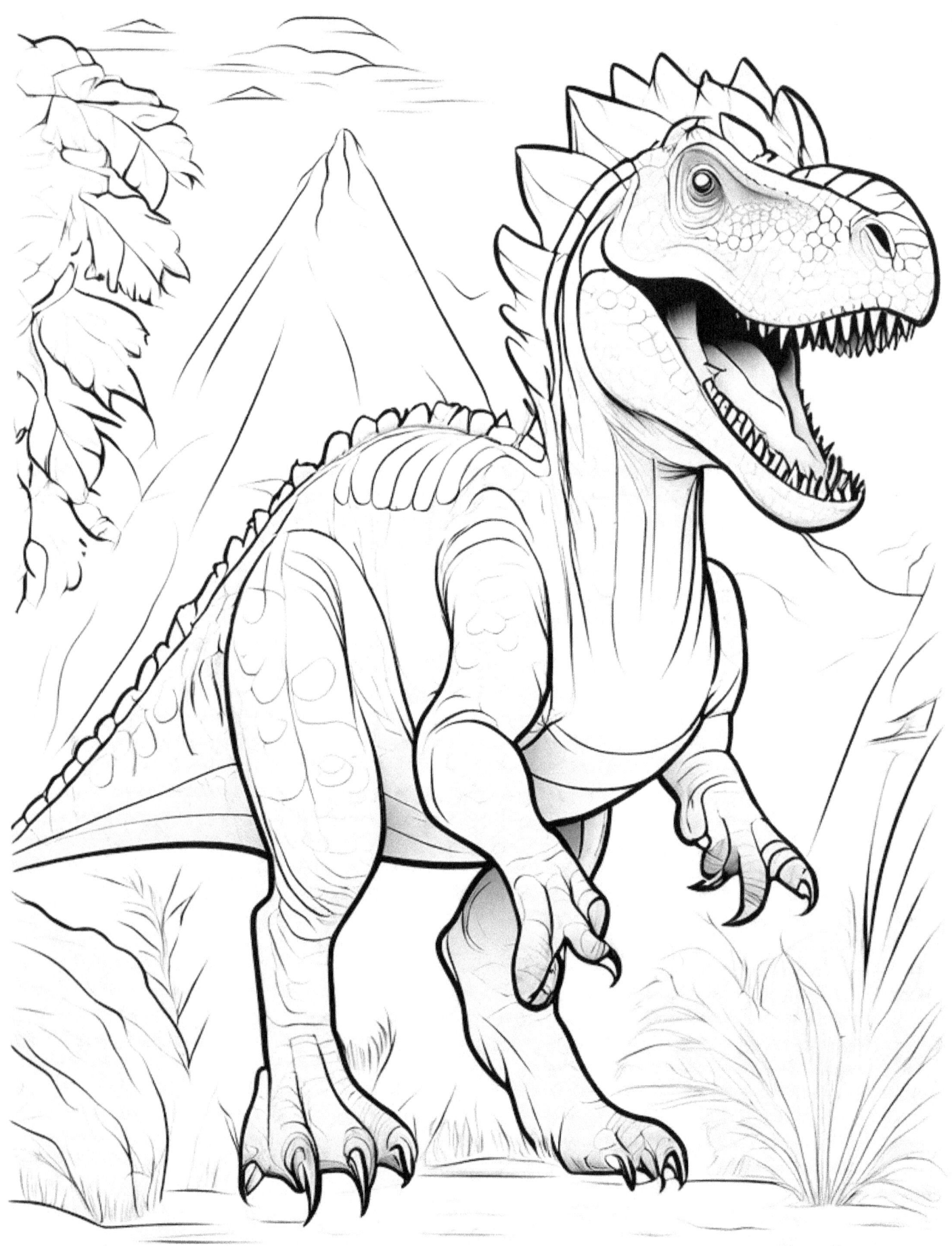

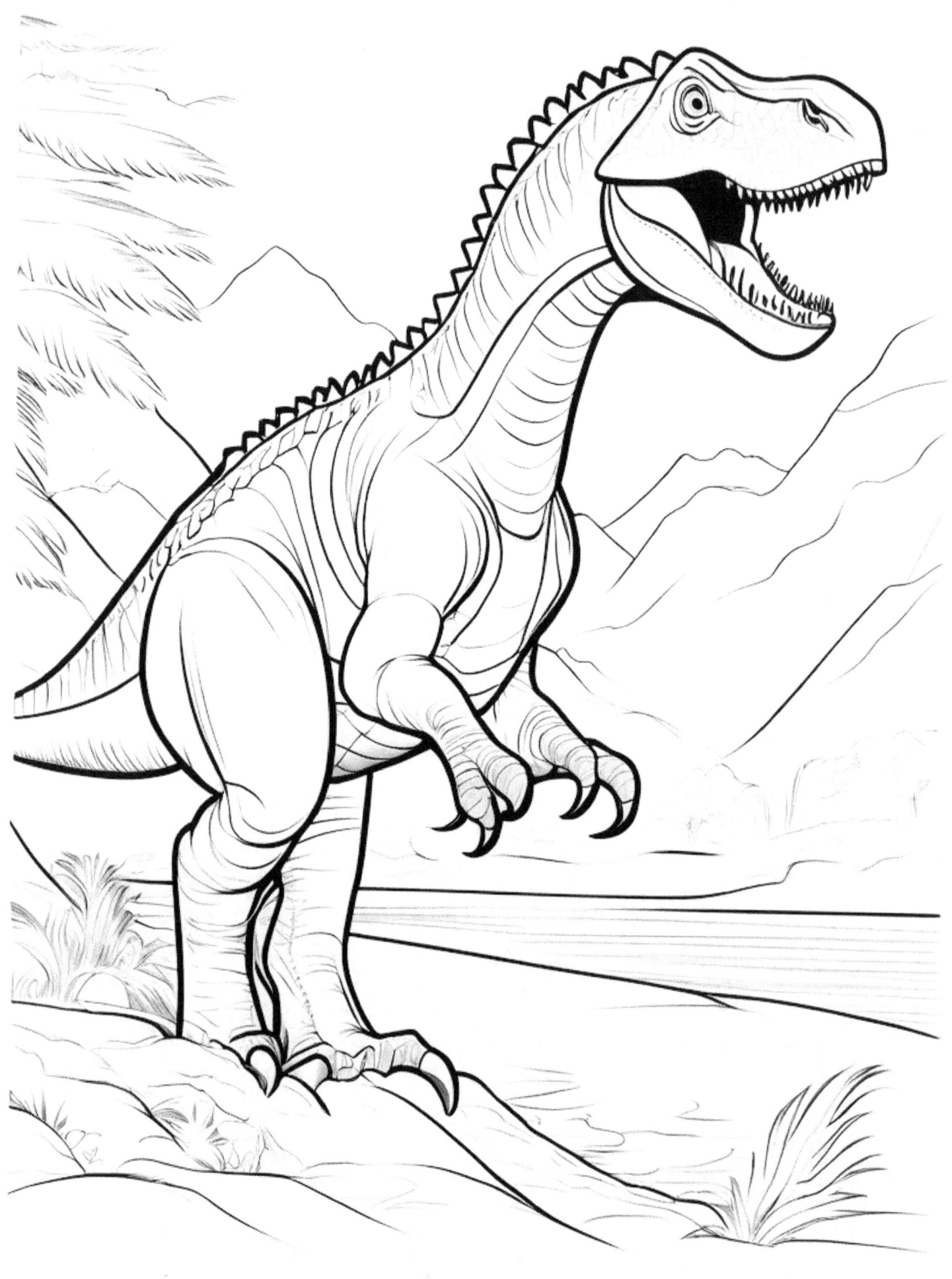

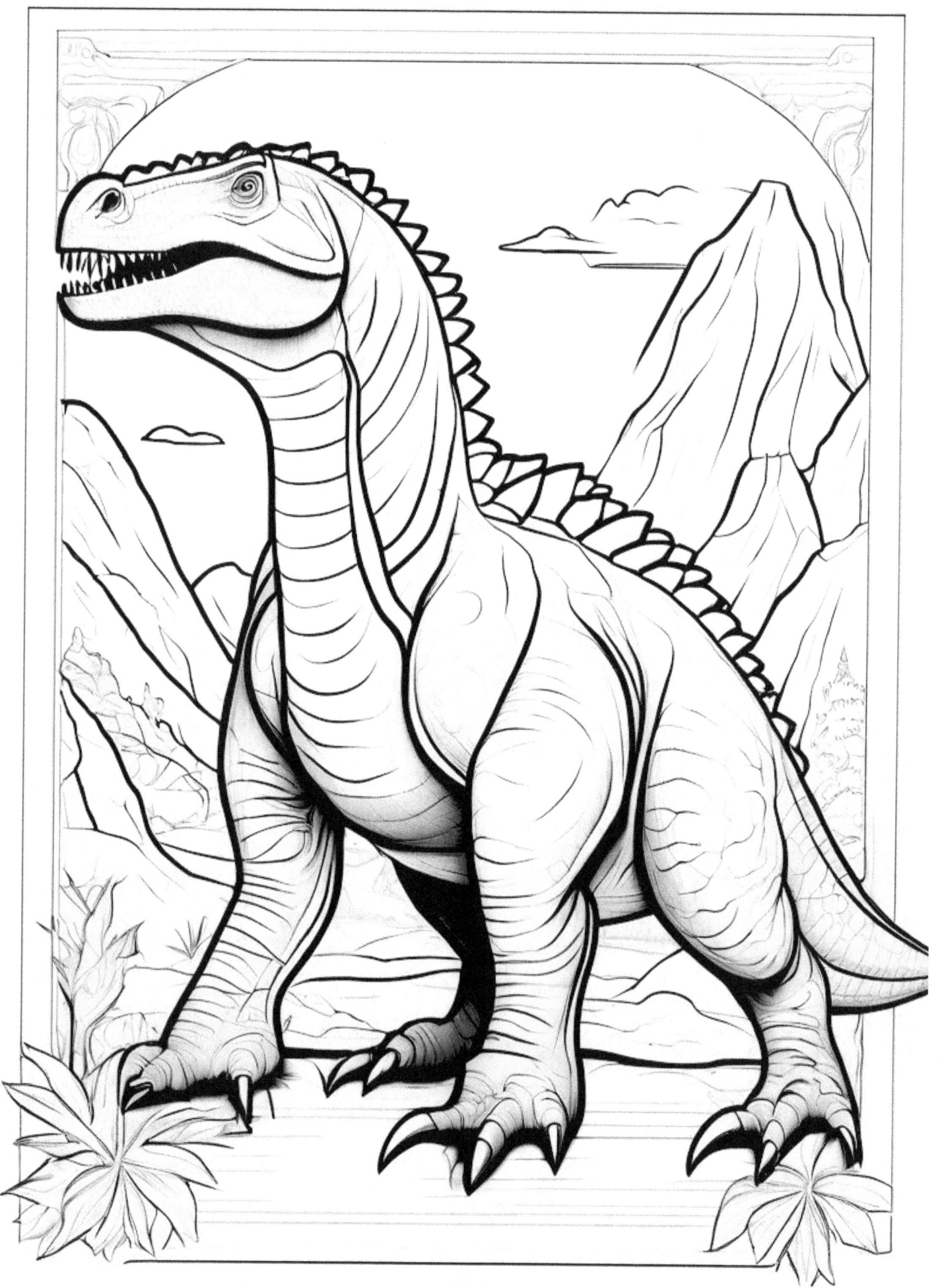

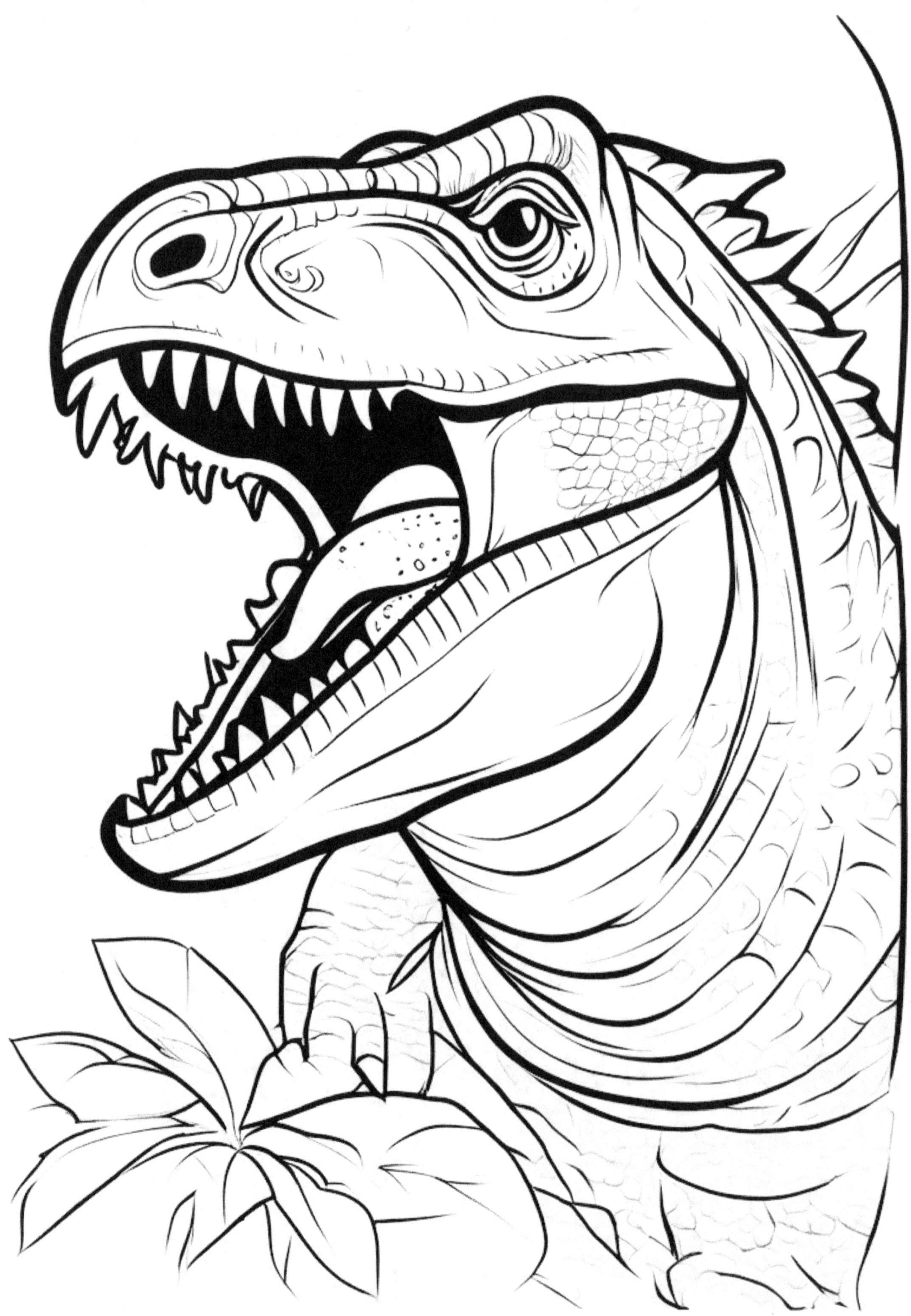

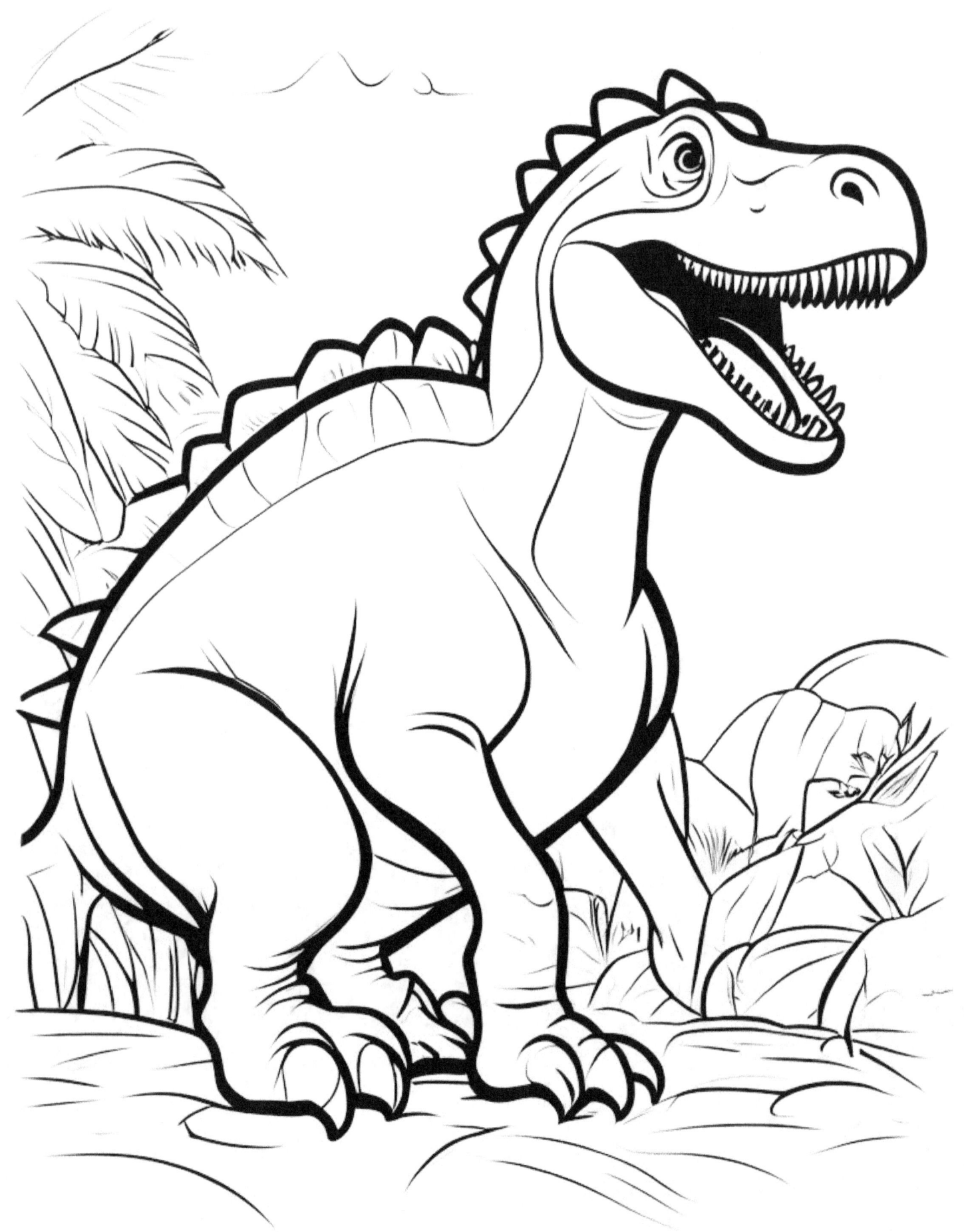

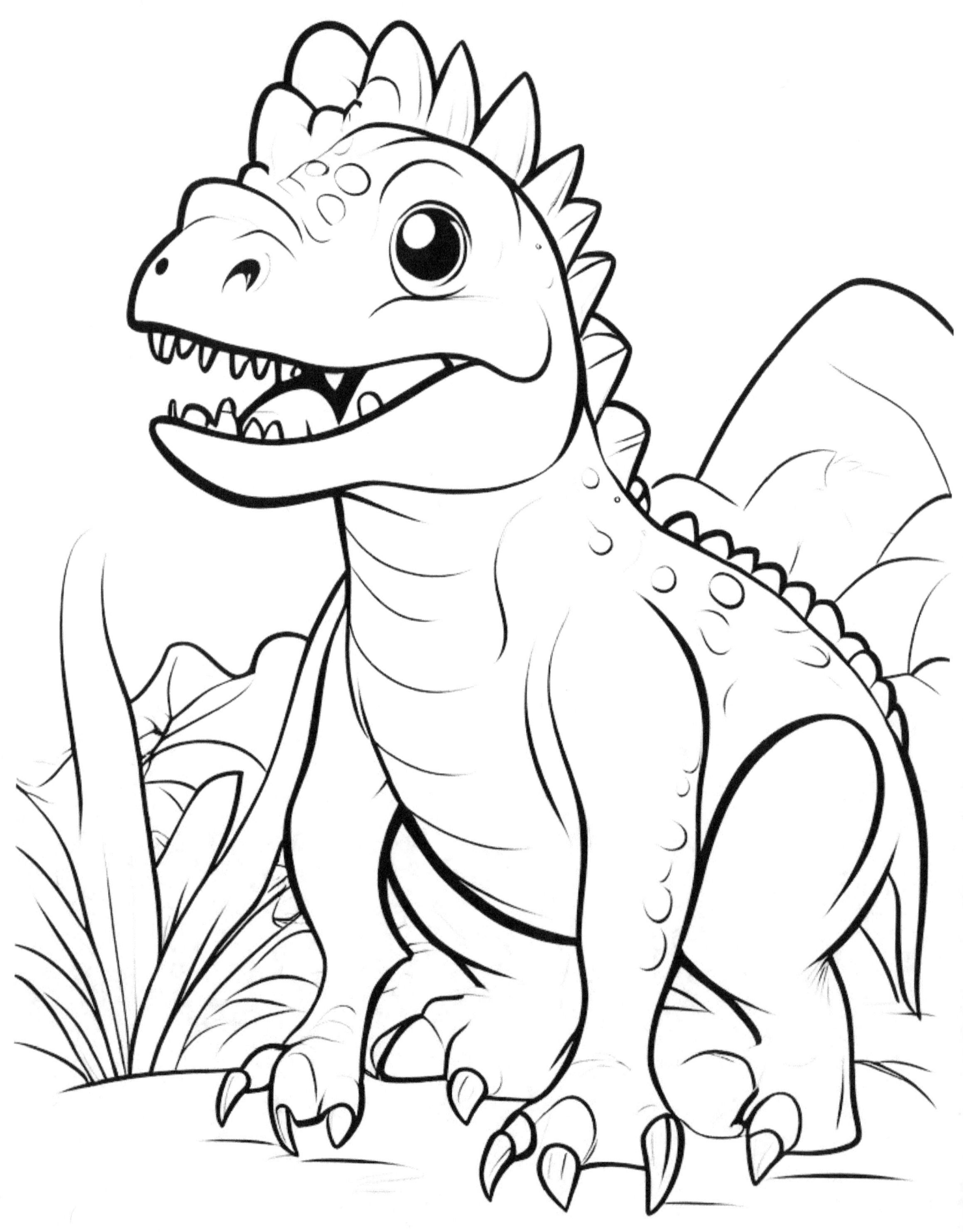

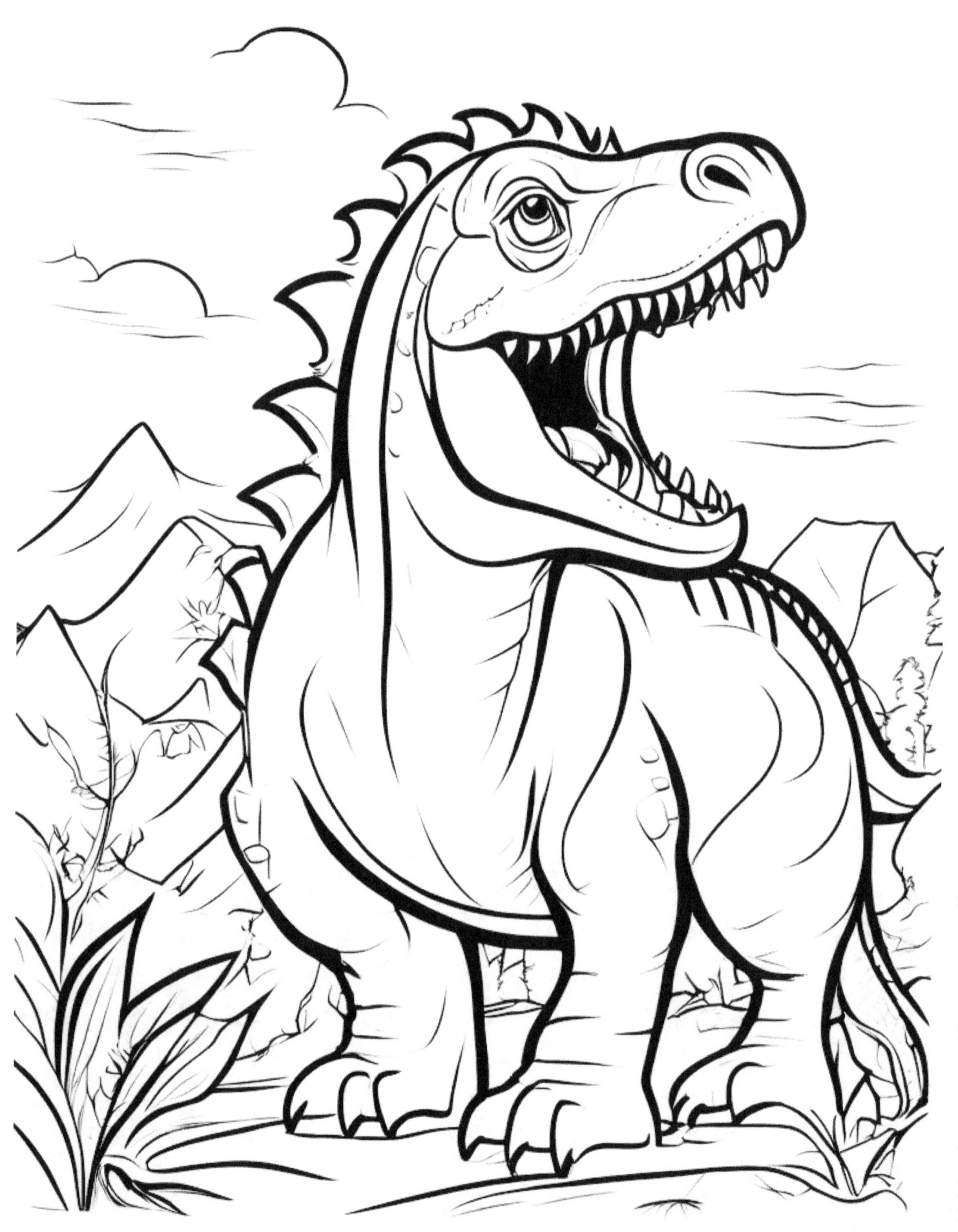

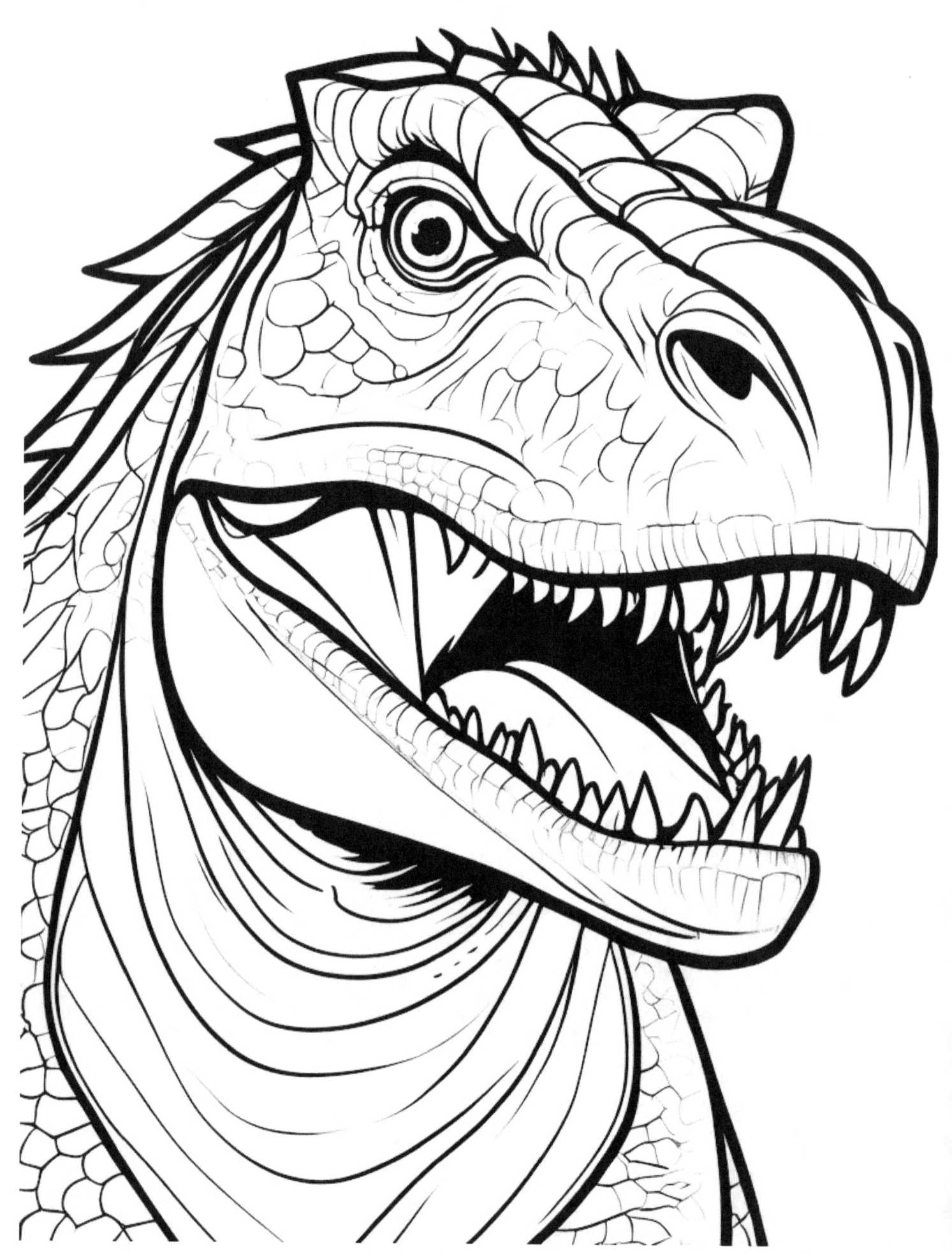

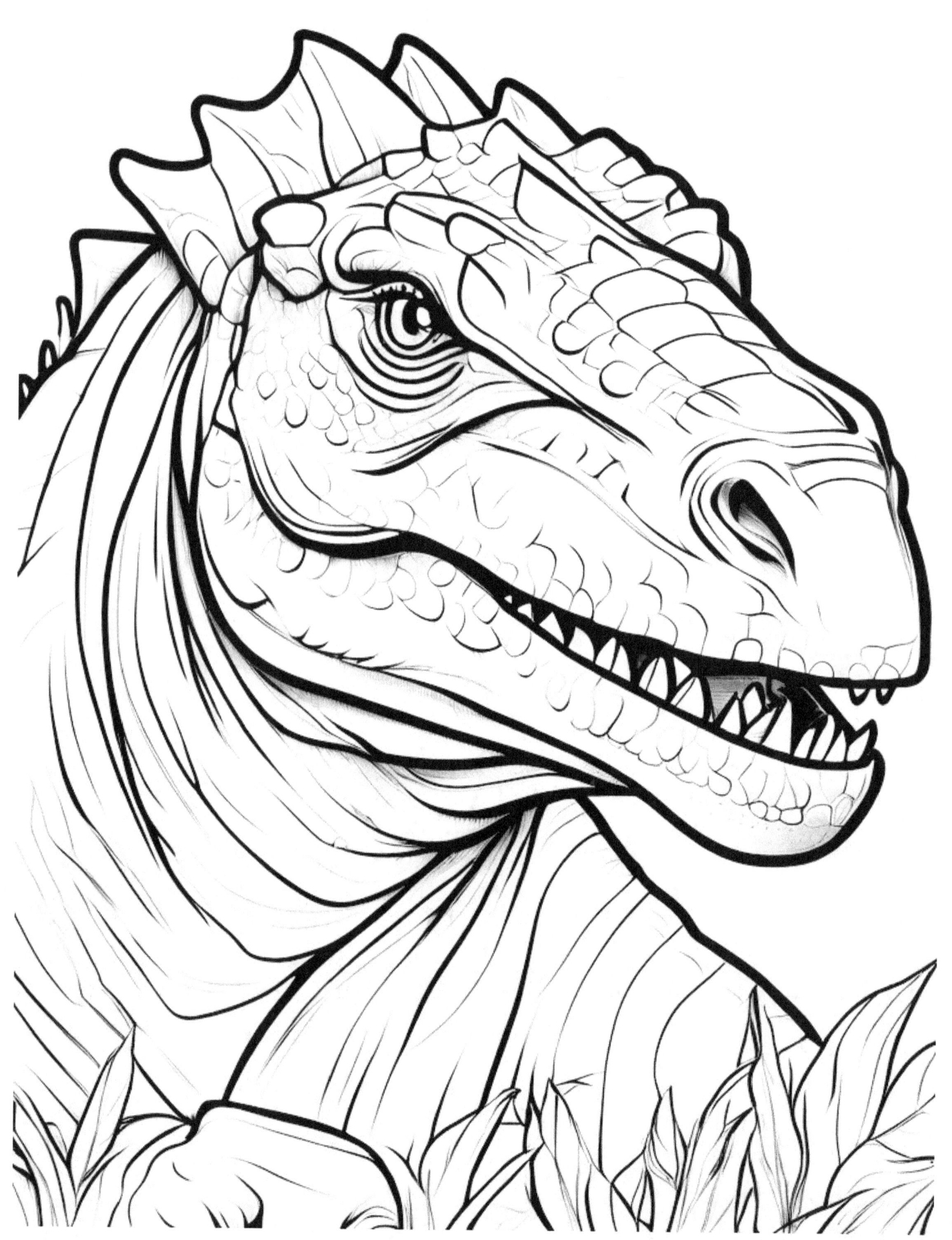

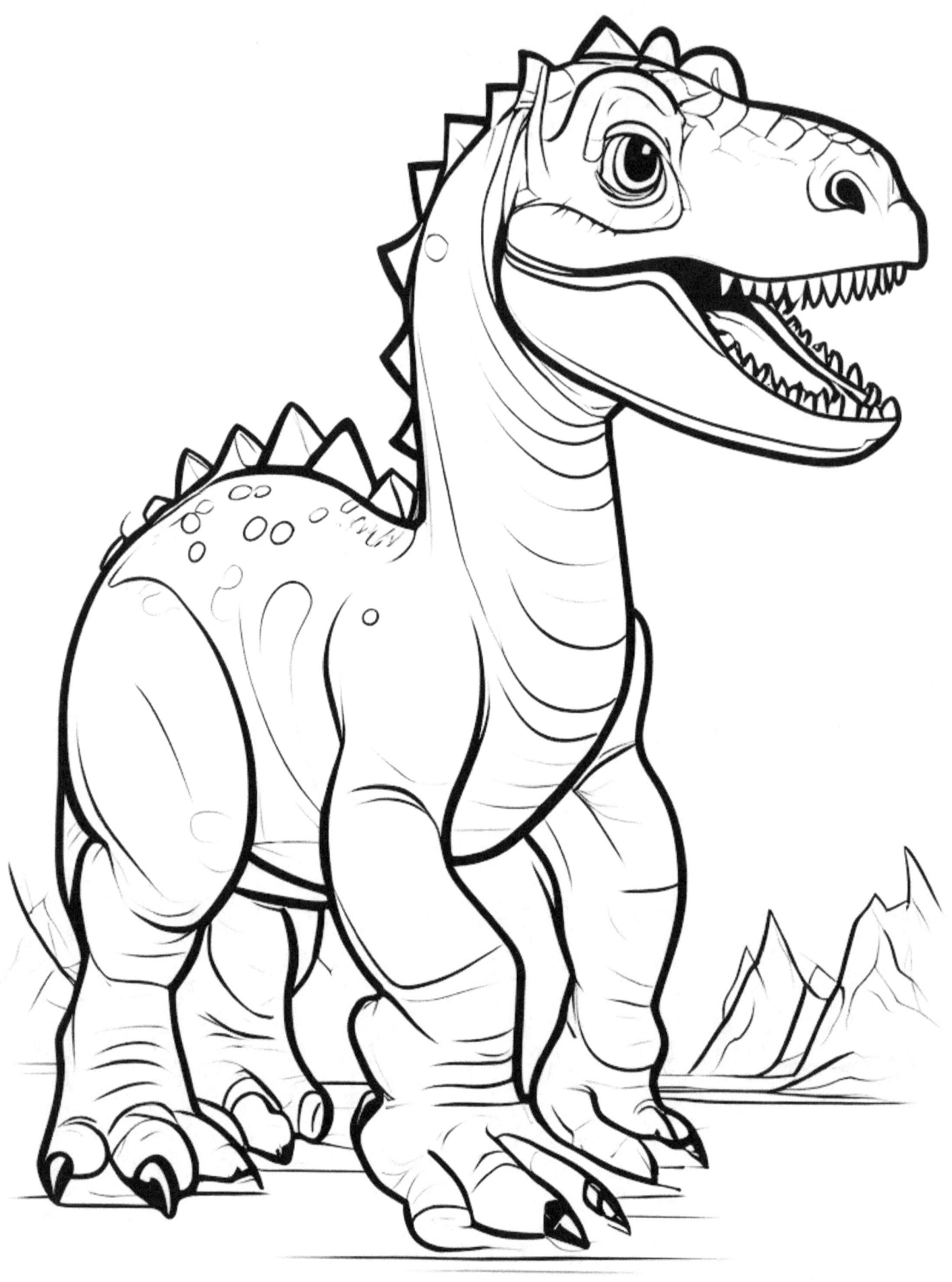

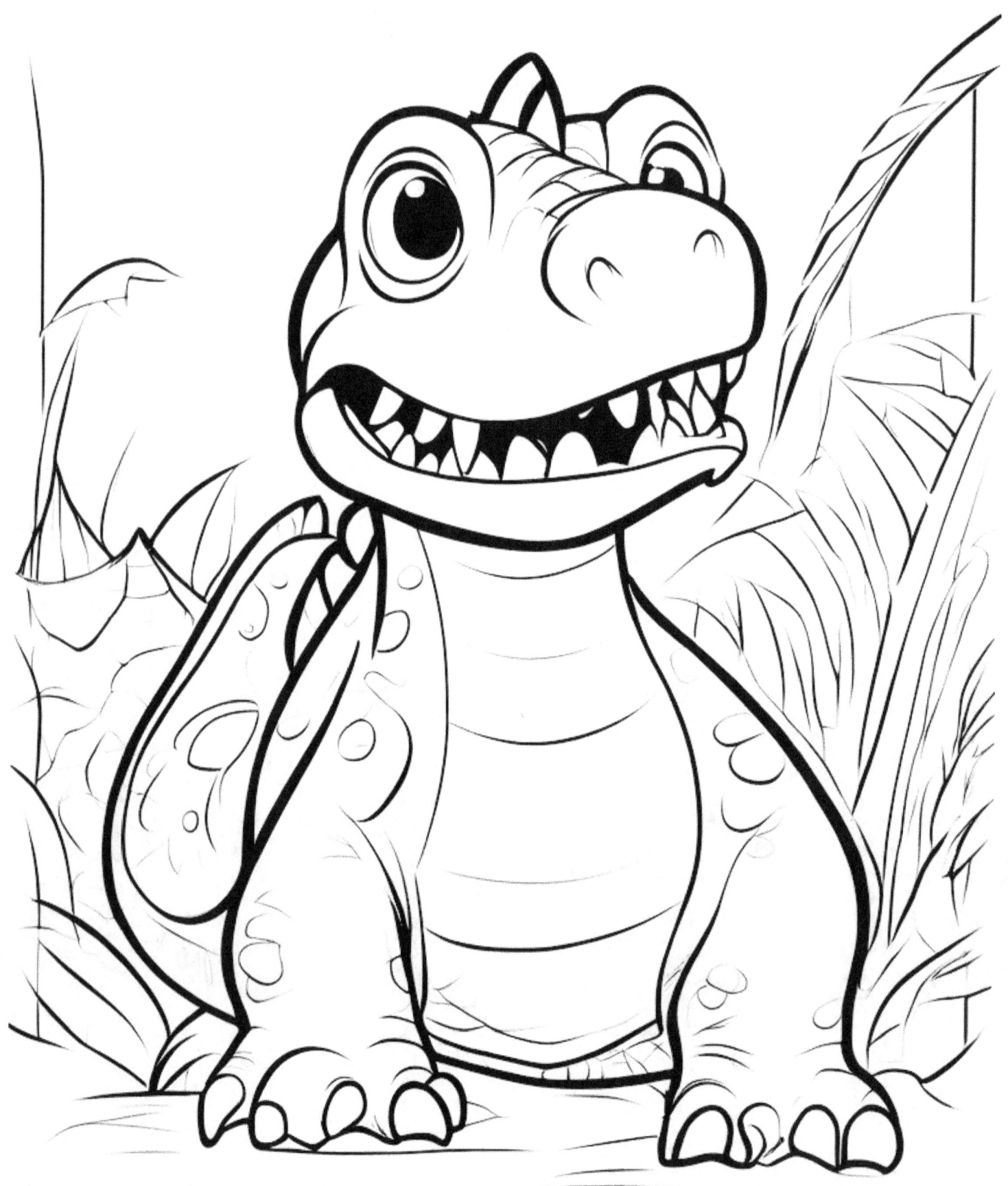

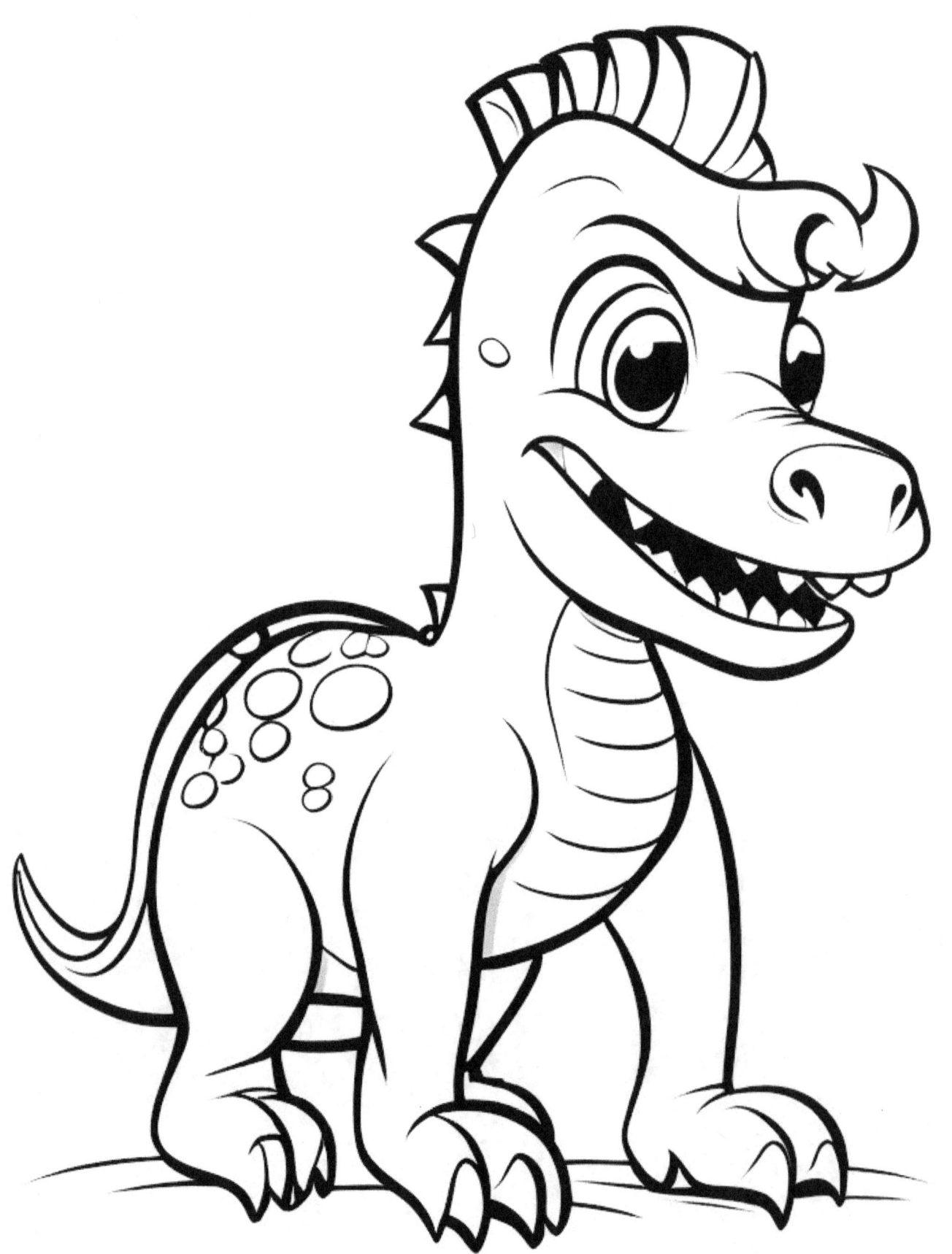

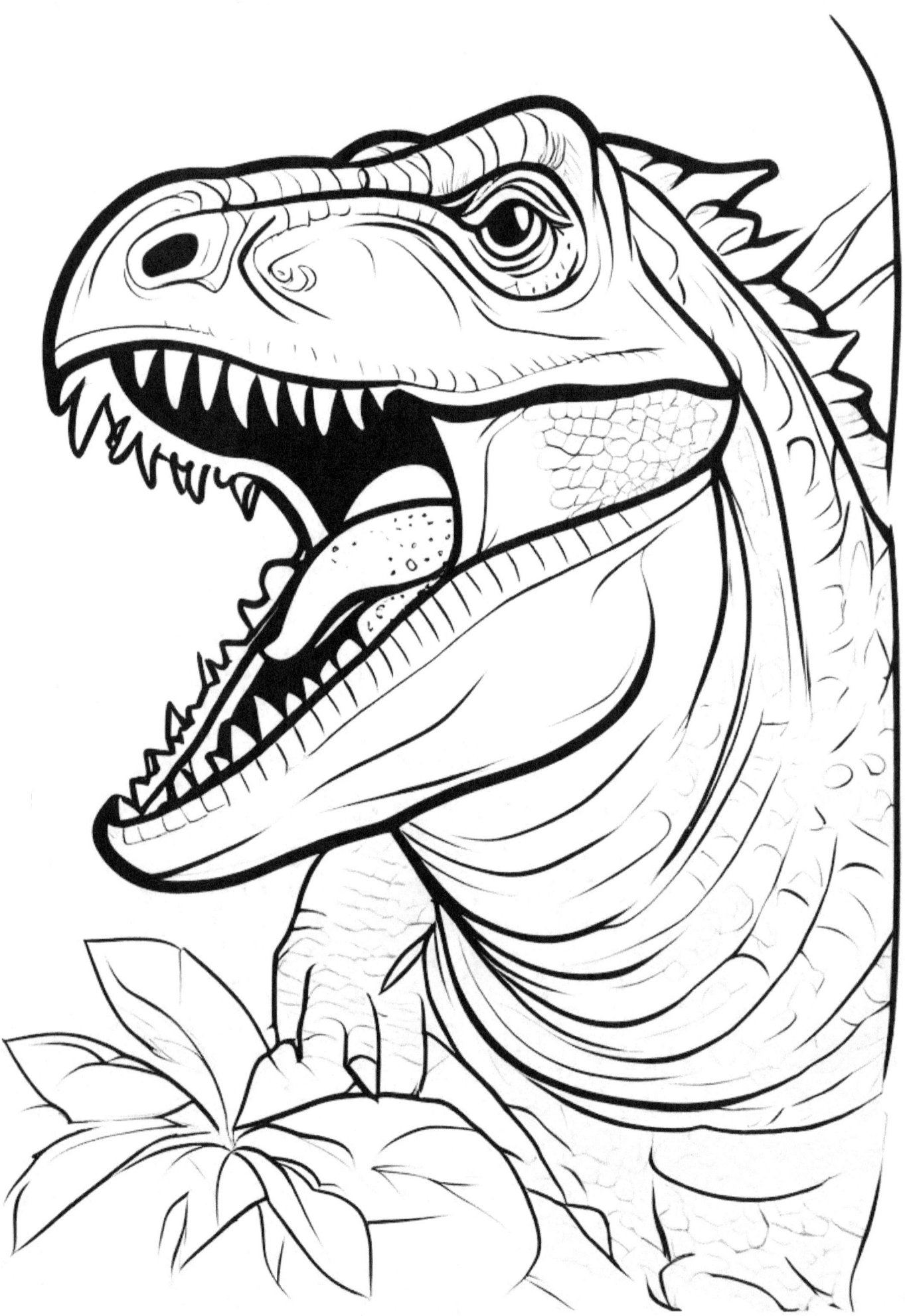

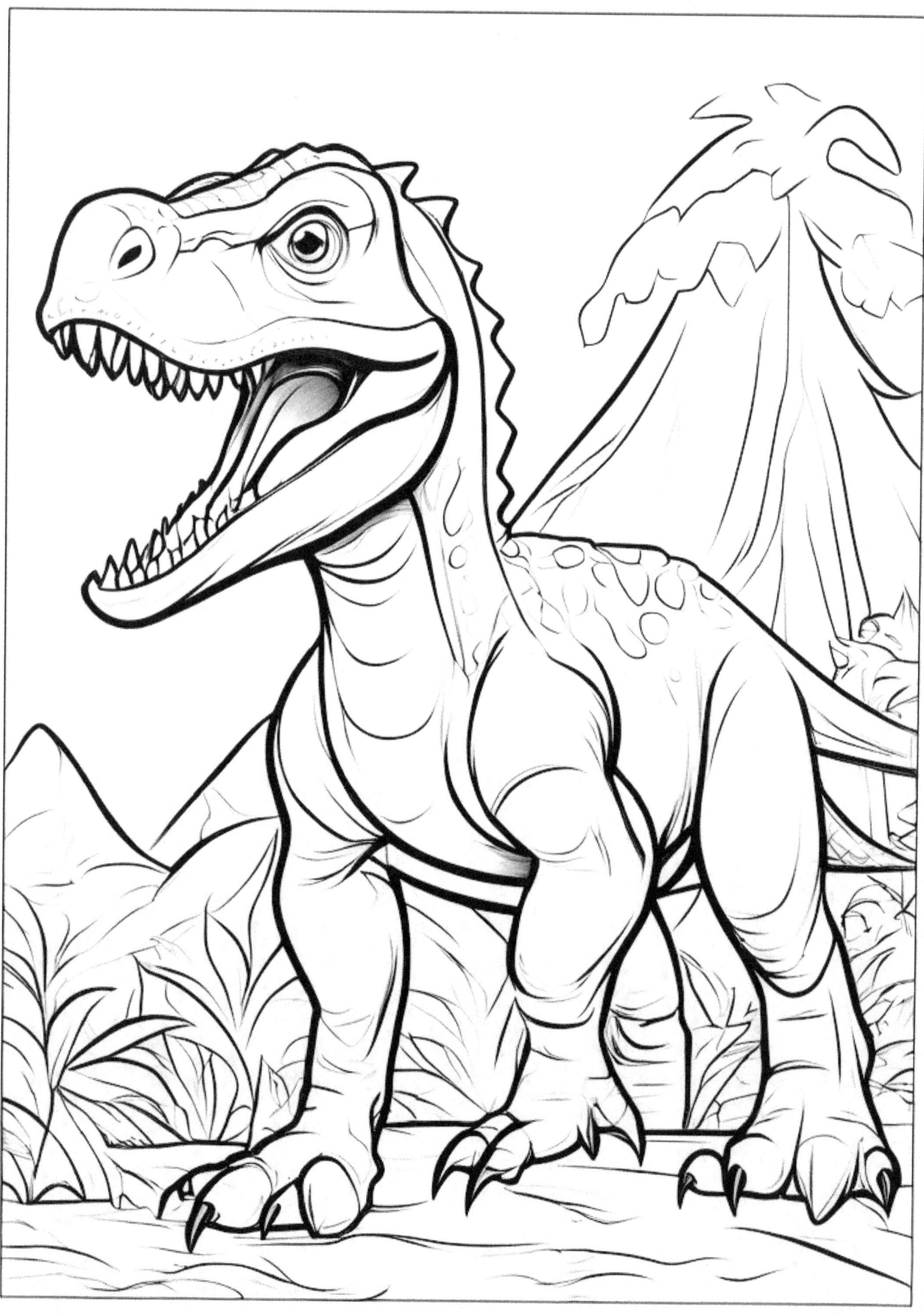

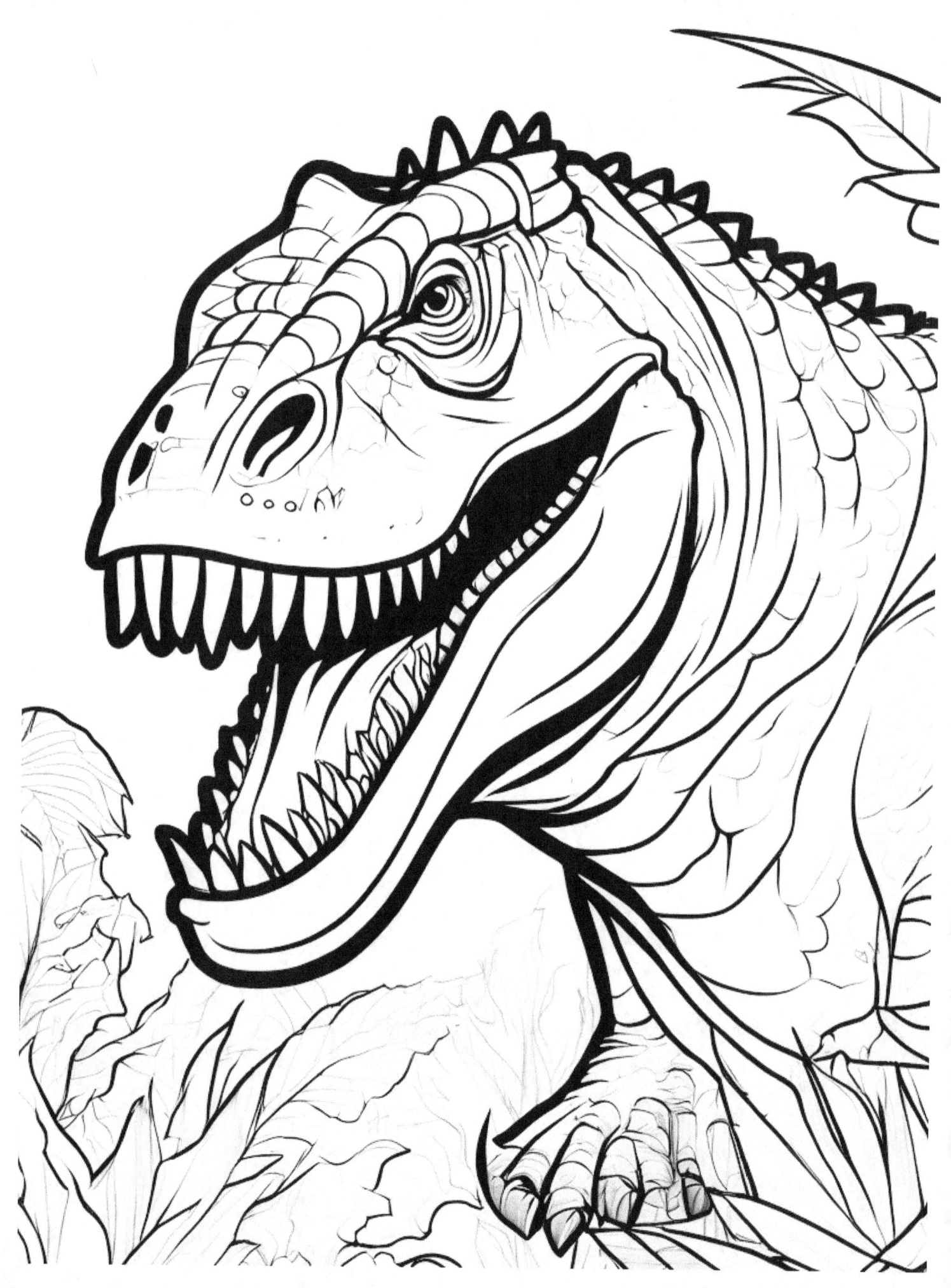

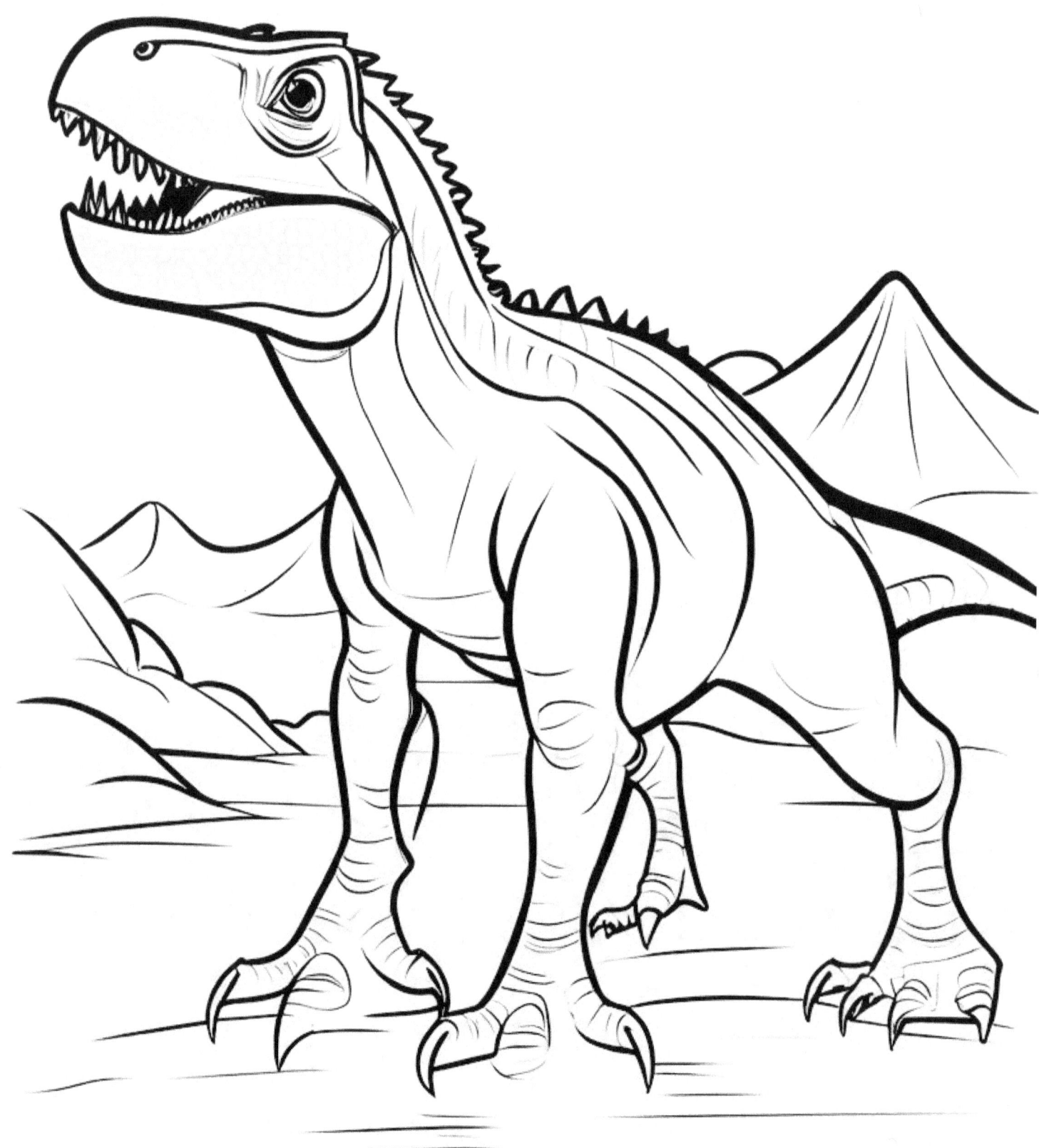

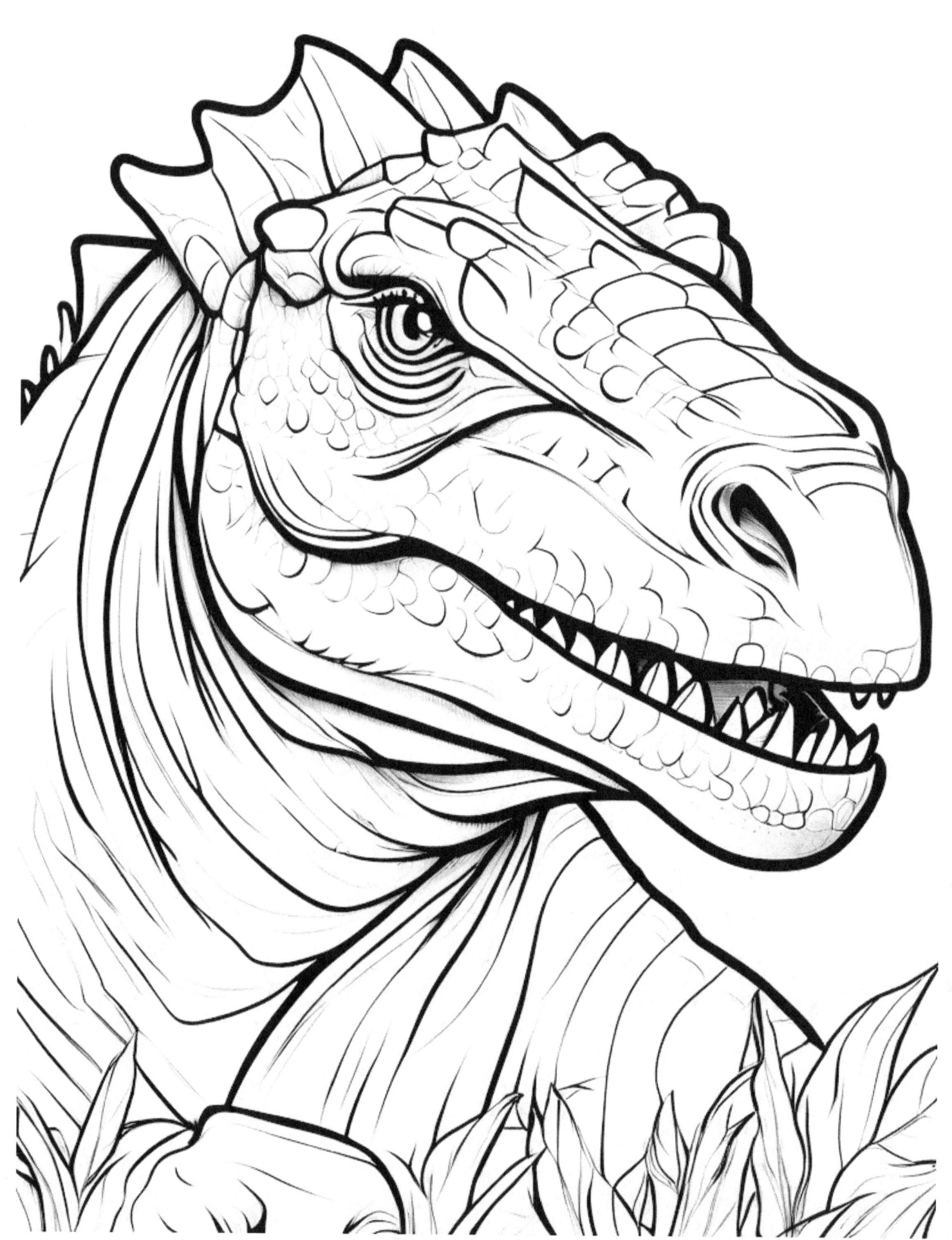